"I highly recommend this real-life page turner! It is a fascinating behind the scenes look at one man's successful mission to integrate the latest technology and training to activate an elite international network of first responders who are achieving more and quicker safe returns of some of our populations most vulnerable citizens who wander."

—Mara Botonis, Best-Selling Author, *When Caring Takes Courage*

"An absolute must read for anyone who is concerned about the health and welfare of people who are subject to wandering regardless of whether or not they know someone who is suffering from a cognitive condition and subject to wandering. The existence of Project Lifesaver International should be broadcast to everybody to ensure universal awareness of the program and the truly lifesaving opportunities it offers to members in every community. With a 30-year career in the SEAL community that included command of SEAL TEAM SIX, I whole heartedly support the mission and goals of Project Lifesaver International especially since the organization's motto of 'Bringing Loved Ones Home' very closely equates to the SEAL motto of 'Never Leave a Man Behind.'"

—Ronald Everest Yeaw, Captain US Navy (Retired)

"I really enjoyed the read! I am one that appreciates [other's] tenacity and concern for those with cognitive issues. I am a parent of a disabled child, and I too have led a search for an autistic child that turned out bad. I appreciate the willingness of Project Lifesaver to assist without hesitation. Project Lifesaver is truly a ray of hope in a world of misunderstanding, confusion and desperation to those parents who have 'elopers'. Thanks Gene and Project Lifesaver family."

—Buddy Williams, Chief of Police, Live Oak Police Department (FL)

"Inspiring! I can now appreciate the total drive, commitment and passion that has made Project Lifesaver such a god-send to so many people impacted by wandering or elopement due to cognitive issues. The book provides a wonderful insight into the journey taken to realize a dream to save lives."

—Mark Mackin, Senior Sergeant, Western Australia Police Force

"*Deploying High* is a fun and insightful book on the life and drive of Chief Gene Saunders. The book will make you look at your own life analyzing what gives you purpose, brings a calmness to your life and makes you feel filled. Thank God for leaders like Chief Saunders who brought us Project Lifesaver."

—Lori La Bey, CEO & Founder, Alzheimer's Speaks

Deploying High:

*The Man, the Mission, and the Story Behind
Project Lifesaver International, the Leading Force in Special-Focus
Search-and-Rescue for the Cognitively Impaired*

by Nora Firestone

© Copyright 2019 Nora Firestone

ISBN 978-1-63393-863-2

Published by

210 60th Street
Virginia Beach, VA 23451
800–435–4811
www.koehlerbooks.com

DEPLOYING HIGH

the man, the mission, and the story behind

PROJECT LIFESAVER INTERNATIONAL

the leading force in special-focus

search-and-rescue for the cognitively impaired

NORA FIRESTONE

VIRGINIA BEACH
CAPE CHARLES

TABLE OF CONTENTS

FOREWORD

The Rewards and Satisfaction of a Lifetime of Public Service

*By Gene Saunders, CEO and
founder of Project Lifesaver International*

T here are many individuals in this world who spend their whole life in search of a purpose, desperately seeking meaningful ways to make a difference in the world with the short amount of time they are given. I consider myself quite lucky, though; I discovered my purpose early in life through a passion to serve and protect.

"The purpose of human life is to serve, and to show compassion and the will to help others."—Albert Schweitzer

My career has brought me in many different directions throughout my life. From my service in the U.S. military to my decorated career in law enforcement, I took on many different roles and ascended through the ranks to positions of leadership. Yet through it all, two things always remained the same: my concern for others' well-being and my dedication to serve my fellow man. During much of that time, however, it was unbeknownst to me that my greatest achievement, potentially my true purpose, was yet to come.

In 1999, while I was serving as Chief of Search and Rescue at the Chesapeake Sheriff's Office in Virginia, and after it became apparent that there was a void in a first responder's ability to provide exceptional search, rescue, and protection to non-cognitive populations prone to elopement, I founded Project Lifesaver. The program was aimed at reducing the recovery times for lost Alzheimer's patients by using electronic search methods in an effort to return these individuals home safely.

While it began as a localized pilot program, news of the program quickly spread throughout surrounding communities. Its innovation in the field and proven success drove its expansion to other agencies. Soon, this entity that I had created was a hot commodity, and to keep up with its rapid growth, I retired from my law-enforcement career, after thirty-three years of service, to take on a new role as Project Lifesaver CEO.

Today, Project Lifesaver International is a widely known 501(C)(3) community-based public-safety non-profit organization that provides law enforcement, fire/rescue and other first responders across the globe with a comprehensive search and rescue program designed to safeguard the special-needs community from the life-threatening behavior of wandering.

Experts estimate that more than five million people have Alzheimer's disease in America alone, with these numbers expected to triple in the years to come. Wandering, or elopement, is common among individuals diagnosed with Alzheimer's disease and can be one of the most dangerous behaviors an Alzheimer's patient can present. It is estimated that sixty to seventy percent of all people with Alzheimer's will wander away from safety at least once during the course of their illness. Many will wander six to eight times before they are placed into a residential facility, or until an outside, qualified caretaker is brought into the home to help.

Additionally, the Centers for Disease Control and Prevention estimate that an average of one in fifty-nine children in the U.S. has autism, which can cause significant social, communication and behavioral challenges. These challenges often present unique safety risks, including those associated with the tendency to wander or elope. In fact, data published in *Pediatrics*, the official journal of the American Academy of Pediatrics, estimates that forty-nine percent of children with autism will attempt to elope from a safe environment. Also, a recent National Autism Association survey concluded that nearly ninety-two percent of parents felt their autistic child was at risk of wandering away and becoming lost.

The task of searching for wandering or lost individuals with autism, Alzheimer's, or other cognitive conditions presents challenges not typically experienced in standard search-and-rescue operations, and with the number of diagnoses dramatically growing each year, wandering is becoming a serious societal problem. Without effective procedures and equipment, searches can involve multiple agencies, hundreds of officers, countless man-hours and tens of thousands of dollars. More importantly, because time is of the essence, every minute lost increases the risk of a tragic outcome. If not located within twenty-four hours, an eloped individual's likelihood of being located without significant injury decreases by fifty percent, and time is of even greater importance in the instance of a missing individual with autism, as many of these individuals have an attraction to and fascination with water. This attraction, coupled with their inability to detect danger, means that many children on the autism spectrum who wander will likely head straight to a nearby body of water. And current statistics indicate that drowning is the leading cause of autism-related wandering deaths.

Project Lifesaver, now the gold standard in the field, was the first organization to significantly address the elopement issue among at-risk individuals, as well as the first to apply locating technology for the search and rescue of these individuals. Our clear and singular focus is on providing the needed support, protection, and peace of mind to one of society's most vulnerable groups and their caregivers, while also delivering the tools and training to public safety agencies that respond to incidents of elopement.

The method relies on proven radio technology and specially trained search-and-rescue teams. Individuals enrolled in Project Lifesaver wear a small personal transmitter around the wrist or ankle that emits an individualized tracking signal. If an enrolled client goes missing, the caregiver notifies local authorities who will dispatch a certified emergency response team to the client's last known location, and activate a search with specialized equipment to triangulate the position of the client's frequency, allowing the team to quickly locate the client and return them home safely.

In comparison to a search using standard operations, which can take hours or possibly days, Project Lifesaver has reduced search times drastically, achieving an average recovery time of only thirty minutes, which is ninety-five percent less time than standard operations.

Now, in nearly 1,600 public-safety agencies internationally, Project Lifesaver has been credited with the successful recovery of more than 3,500 eloped individuals since its founding in 1999. Boasting a 100-percent success rate, Project Lifesaver continues to achieve its mission of "bringing loved ones home!"

What makes our approach unique is that Project Lifesaver is more than just wearable locating technology; it is a *program*. We have created an entire training and certification protocol targeted at public-safety agencies that includes not only search-and-rescue techniques and the use of our equipment, but also educational programs to provide these officers with critical insight into the disorders they will be working with, including the latest health information related to these conditions and how best to approach and communicate with these individuals. Engaging these professionals in such topics helps them build relationships with, and gain the trust of, their clients and other special needs community members, and enables them to more effectively interact with these individuals; in the case of elopement, the training enables them to put their clients at ease when returning them home. This training also allows these first responders to better understand behaviors in the field, and it helps them identify, assess, and manage interactions with special-needs individuals throughout regular duties.

Because of our extensive experience in this area of expertise, Project Lifesaver has provided valuable insight and information in the development of policy and sound practices for the search, rescue, and safe recovery of at-risk wanderers. We help in the development of materials and training programs to provide the necessary education to doctors, school administrators, first responders/search personnel, and of course, the families of loved ones at risk. In fact, Project Lifesaver is a subject matter expert and advisor on the wandering issue for: Leaders Engaged on Alzheimer's disease (LEAD); National Center for Missing & Exploited Children; The International Association of Chiefs of Police (IACP); Alzheimer's Foundation; and the National Alzheimer's Project Act (NAPA). The Project Lifesaver training program is recognized and approved by the Virginia Department of Criminal Justice Services and National Preparedness Institute of Indian River State College.

Most importantly though, the Project Lifesaver program has provided a means of protection and an additional layer of security for these individuals should they wander, as well as tremendous peace of mind for their families. No matter how watchful and diligent a caregiver is, their loved one is still likely to display this life-threatening behavior, and I am proud to provide an option to keep them safe.

Establishing this program and growing it to the size and notoriety that it is today has not always been an easy road, but this by far has been one of the most rewarding things I have done in my life. Project Lifesaver has far exceeded my expectations, especially given that developing this program was never something I sought. I simply wanted to serve and protect, and in that, I found a match of inspiration waiting to be lit that would soon ignite the fire that would forever change the search-and-rescue industry.

Achieving this success was certainly not single-handed, though, and while it was attained under my leadership, I have had an incredible staff that played a critical role in the organization's continued success. Every single employee has a passion for the populations we serve and a stake in the organization's success, each providing ideas, strengths, and direction to ensure the continuity of the organization and this life-saving program. We are a mission-driven team and we always put collective goals ahead of individual glory. We succeed because we are a small but nimble organization that rises to any challenge we face. Everyone at Project Lifesaver is smart, energetic, and fun to work with. We love what we do, and it shows in the strong relationships we have built with our clients, member agencies, and strategic partners.

Project Lifesaver is more than just a job; it is a way of life because, at the end of the day, there is more at stake than a paycheck. We work each day to safeguard lives, and together, we have made a difference.

The accomplishments of this organization continue to amaze me each and every day, and I hope that we can continue on this path of greatness and one day be able to provide this program free of cost to everyone in need, ending the fatalities and injuries caused by special-needs elopement.

PREFACE AND
ACKNOWLEDGMENTS

I first met Chief Gene Saunders and his wife, Jean O. Saunders, around 2008 when, as a reporter, I wrote an article about Project Lifesaver International, the leading force in search and rescue for people prone to wandering due to cognitive impairments, for *The Virginian-Pilot* newspaper. Following numerous interviews and what research I conducted for the article, and having gotten to know Chief Saunders during the process, I became indelibly impressed by the man and his mission, what he and his team had been achieving, and the far-reaching impact the small organization that he had founded here in southeastern Virginia had grown to have on countless people throughout North America.

After that article ran, Saunders and I stayed in touch. We more than toyed with the thought of writing a book about PLI, but the timing must not have been divine.

In 2016, when Mike Herron, publisher of *Inside Leadership* magazine, asked his writer/reporters for suggestions about people and organizations to feature in future issues, I highly recommended Saunders and Project Lifesaver International. Herron agreed, and I interviewed Gene and Jean again, as well as several others—PLI staff, agents, volunteers and client/beneficiaries of the program—for the 3,000-plus-word article that ran that December.

By then, I was hooked again on the value of this awe-inspiring organization, the sense of purpose and mission carried by the people who operate and support it, and the incredible vision, drive and tenacity of its founder and CEO, Chief Gene Saunders. Since its inception, through its wild expansion and the hellish years of sabotage and betrayals by trusted associates, PLI has established approximately 1,600 agencies and completed more than 3,500 search-and-rescue events throughout North America.

Through all the ups, downs, challenges and rewards, Saunders deployed the leadership style and skills he had cultivated throughout his lifetime of service and teamwork—from his early years in scouting through his extensive career in military, law-enforcement and search-and-rescue fields. Through it all, he relied on the invaluable faith and assistance of his wife, his closest supporters and his biggest cheerleaders.

I learned more than I can summarize here about life and leadership from Saunders and his story, and I hope to have effectively conveyed the heart of it in "Deploying High." It was my pleasure and honor to write the story of this amazing ongoing mission and the people who continue to make the inroads that save the lives of those who cannot help themselves.

Thanks to my family and friends, who always mean the world to me, and in this case especially to my parents, Karen Wahl and Ed Wahl; my brothers, Ed, Tim and Matt Wahl, and their families; my children, Aaron, Evan and Eve Firestone; friends and business associates who helped sustain me in ways they might not even realize: publishers John Koehler and Joe Coccaro, editor Marshall McClure, Paula and Larry Cobb, Drew and Mary Ella Nickell, Jacquie Whitt, Laura Hamway, Dr. Alan Krasnoff, Mary Holt, Val Angrosini, Petey Browder, Rebecca Reid and all the members of The Detonators band, whose music and energy fueled my spirit: Michelle King, Rich Grado, Ron Subeh, Jack King and David Lewis Geiger; and Victoria Hecht, my first and longtime editor at *The Virginian-Pilot*, whose assignment introduced me to Saunders and PLI, and without whom I might have carried my writing aspirations to my grave without ever having realized them within the life-changing realm of journalism and professional writing that I so love today.

Thanks to all the Project Lifesaver International staff, agents, volunteers and clients who contributed their insights and stories, including Tommy Carter, Rick Derus, Paul Ballance, Martha

Lieberman, Amber Williams, Bob Smith, Gayle Schultz and Kyrianna Hoffses. Without their input, I'd have had to make the whole thing up!

Most of all, thanks to Chief Gene Saunders and his wife, Jean Saunders, for all you do and all you have shared for the telling of your story. I am proud to know you, and it is an honor to have finally written this book as you celebrate 20 years of absolutely awe-inspiring accomplishments in the field of special-focus search and rescue for those most vulnerable members of our communities across the continent.

Congratulations on an ongoing mission superbly executed.

ONE

Caught in a Storm

*"My son is a vibrant free spirit, full of imagination and wonder.
His autism sometimes leads to unexpected journeys."*

—*Gayle Schultz, mother of Bob Smith*

Virginia Beach, Virginia, 2016

B ob Smith sat safe at home on a seasonally gray October
morning, snug between the receding oceanfront chill and
the breaking sun. Only when his smile returned with a gentle
reveal was it obvious it had ever waned.

The man's vibrant paintings adorn the path to a bedroom
closetful. They're documentation of his memories, like photographs
are to others, and reflect his wide-eyed view of the world.

"The Beach" blazes thick, impressionistic strokes of ocean and
sky surrounded by red sand. "Carnival with Roller Coasters and
Rides" chronicles a day at Busch Gardens in nearby Williamsburg.
"A Park and Playground for Kids" lends a purposeful acrylic sprawl
to the generally overlooked.

Smith, thirty-four, seeks beauty in nature and people, and he'll
wander far to find it. His memory serves him well come painting
time, but not always along the journey.

Words evaded him as he tried to recall swimming as a toddler
with his Nana and Uncle Wooley–back when he'd been considered
an "advanced communicator" because he'd started talking prior to

his first birthday; sometime before age three, when he'd stopped speaking and begun staring; before the autism diagnosis that had swung normalcy 180 degrees and the symptoms progressed quickly, all according to his mom, Gayle Schultz.

Everything Smith sees is vivid, Schultz noted; "everything is intensified." She sat cross-legged on the carpet, sipping coffee and retelling intense, colorful stories of her own: panic-wrought recollections of the countless times her son had gone missing since the family had moved cross-country to southeastern Virginia's Hampton Roads region in 1990.

"My son is a vibrant free spirit, full of imagination and wonder," she began. "His autism sometimes leads to unexpected journeys."

She emphasized "the three big events," their once-harsh edges now softened by an underlying assurance that Project Lifesaver International, a locally founded search-and-rescue initiative for people prone to wandering due to cognitive disorders, has had their backs since just after the first of them.

That was in 2003 when, savoring his semi-independent status, Smith bicycled aimlessly away from his rented room despite foreboding weather. As twilight ebbed to obscurity, the same rain that lulled others cozy beneath surrounding rooftops descended upon Smith—lost, exposed and confused—with an inescapable ruthlessness.

"All night he rode his bike," Schultz recalled. "He went to people's houses to ask for help, and no one would help him."

The next morning, a man phoned Schultz. "Bob was standing in the man's driveway, exhausted from riding his bike all night," Schultz recounted. The caller had been astute enough to suspect Smith of needing assistance rather than suspect him of malicious intent, and fortunately he'd succeeded in drawing reliable contact information from the twenty-one-year-old.

The man fed Smith a sandwich before Schultz and her husband, Keith Schultz, retrieved their adventuresome son.

Scary as the event was, it could have been worse. In fact, it often is. The family needed help.

(The story above is an excerpt from an article written by Nora Firestone and first published in *Inside Leadership* magazine Vol. 2, No. 4.)

TWO

The Nature of a Beast

*"There's been a lot of work done since that time . . .
but still, it's a 'SWAG'-A scientific, wild-ass guess."*

*—Chief Gene Saunders, regarding traditional
search-and-rescue procedure*

S uch scenarios wreak havoc every day for children and adults with intellectual and cognitive impairments ranging from autism and Down syndrome to traumatic brain injury, dementia and others. They're the source of growing issues that had so rattled Chief Gene Saunders, perhaps one of Hampton Roads' most visionary and ambitious law-enforcement agents of his generation, back in 1999, when he began cultivating what has since become the leading force in North America and beyond for its type of special-focus expedited search and rescue.

"I started Project Lifesaver as a result of failure," Saunders, founder and CEO, recounted from his Florida office in 2017. The colors surrounding him represented an array of rank insignias and commendations. They told of major accomplishments, but not what it took to achieve them.

His face dulled. One "failure" still haunted him from the niche in his mind where it had settled to snare his conscience twenty-eight years earlier.

Chesapeake, Virginia, May 1989

Greenbrier Country Club's slick greens rose to their debut expectation of professional standards as devotees gathered for the Ladies Professional Golf Association's Crestar Classic tournament.

Saunders, then captain with the Chesapeake Police Department, worked plainclothes crowd- and player-security detail. Also in charge of the CPD's Special Operations Department and overseer of its increasing number of standard search-and-rescue assignments, he received an urgent countermand: Activate his SWAT team to locate a seventy-nine-year-old man with Alzheimer's disease just reported missing somewhere in the city's Western Branch area, across the swell of Elizabeth River that wends north of Great Dismal Swamp.

Saunders knew the hourglass had flipped and that the minute he'd gotten word, he was already behind. As routinely and proficiently as he coordinated search-and-rescue operations, initiating manpower, logistics and search patterns, he also knew the amount of sand in the glass to be finite. And passive though it presented itself, gravity was an aggressor, a wily force with which to contend, as it drew the sand to pile higher and heavier and discharged itself by the pressure to unfurl as the gravity of the task before him.

That much, he knew. Everything else would be unpredictable. That's the nature of the beast.

Days passed as Saunders' team worked tirelessly, increasing in size and effort despite vacillant Mother Nature and heedless Father Time. After the initial twenty-four to thirty-six hours' "trying to figure out where this fella could have gone," hope of finding the man alive had significantly diminished, Saunders stated upon reflection. "But what you keep hoping is, well, maybe he's gotten in a car, or he's caught a bus or something," he said, "and he's gone somewhere and we just haven't picked up on it yet. So you keep the search going."

The more time passed, the more assets the search involved: dogs, horses, ATVs, helicopters. An initial team of about forty SWAT agents and patrol officers grew nearly tenfold, to comprise some 350 to 400 diligent participants from civilian and public-safety sects.

Meanwhile leads poured in, in the form of reported sightings in neighboring communities and cities.

"You have to follow up on those things," Saunders said. "And you're sending people all over the place. But you're still concentrating within an area, and it's getting bigger and bigger and bigger" with time.

With every area they covered, Saunders wondered if they'd covered well enough. "He could have wandered back into the area, or we could have missed him," Saunders explained. "It's not like that doesn't happen." So they selectively retraced.

Almost two weeks in, immersed in the backtrack, "that's when we found him," Saunders recalled. The team had discovered the body in the warmth of late morning, off a small footpath in a large, overgrown, rough area flecked by stones and debris, only a quarter-mile from where the man's trek had begun.

The slip of Saunders' expression exposed a smoldering frustration. "In one way, you feel relief because we found him," he said. "But in the other, you know . . ." He shook his head. "There's no relief."

In this case, Saunders said, "the best we can figure, he felt like he needed to go to work. He was trying to cross a rough piece of ground almost directly in line with his last employment. In his mind, he had to go to work.

"It really bothered me," he continued, arousing his inner critic. "Why didn't we find him? Well, a lot of things come into your mind: *Did I have enough people? Should I have started somewhere different?*"

Moreover, the lost don't always aid the searchers, Saunders said, and those with cognitive impairments typically can't. They may be unaware of their situation and its potential for danger. Or they may intentionally hide from searchers out of fear, confusion or the sense that they have done something shameful or punishable. "Whether this happened with this gentleman or not, I don't know," Saunders conceded. "I hate to think that we missed him, but can I say that we didn't? No."

The event represented a crippling bullet to the heart of honorable pursuit; a defining building block of an allegorical beast taking shape.

Salting the wound, the radio call to Saunders' command post had announced the man dead on arrival to anyone monitoring it, including members of the media and general civilian public. Discreetness hadn't dawned on that era, and the lack of it helped neither the team's next-step logistics and morale nor public perception of its competence.

Saunders saw no purpose in heading to the scene. He had capable people on site, and they had conveyed the pertinent details. He notified his superiors. Homicide detectives would be summoned to rule out foul play, and several hours' worth of work would transpire before the man would be moved. Saunders had nothing unique to contribute to the process in place; he'd only be in the way. His priority shifted to notifying the family. They had been frequenting the command post, near the house from which the man had wandered.

"I would never delegate that to anybody; I always did it myself," Saunders said of the grueling task. When possible, he'd bring a cleric. "Unfortunately, on this particular search, I don't remember a police chaplain being available. So you just . . . you know, you search for words to say.

"But what are you going to say?" He shrugged. "I mean, what do you say? You just . . .

"I went in, and I told the family that I'm very sorry to report that we have located him, and, unfortunately, the news is not good; he did not survive. And that was it.

"It's a heavy feeling," Saunders said. "You know, why did it have to end this way? And the biggest thing—and I don't know about other guys who command searches, but to me—is this: What did we not do that we should have, that would have caused this to be a good, successful search in which the person was returned safely?

"What did we miss?

"What did *I* not do?

"What did *we* not do?"

Some elements of traditional search-and-rescue procedure haven't changed much since then, Saunders said. "There's been a lot of work done since that time on where you should start and all these kinds of things," he admitted, "but still, it's a 'SWAG:' A *scientific, wild-ass guess.*"

Who really ever escapes the perennial stranglehold of profound defeat? Do-overs are a scantily celebrated luxury of childhood. The best one can do is to transcend. And maybe someday, one-up the beast.

THREE

A Bull Takes Shape

*"I was always bullheaded. If I had something, and
I felt really strongly about it, unless you could give me a
really good, sensible reason not to do it . . ."*

—*Chief Gene Saunders*

A police psychologist once called him an adrenaline junkie—
the kind of person who will wrangle a challenge just to
prove that he can, Saunders reflected. "I guess I would have
to agree," he conceded; it's innate.

Chief Saunders relaxed into his swivel office chair. He'd been up
for two hours, since six a.m. He'd fed the dog, watched some news,
headed to the office, and consumed coffee and three hard-boiled
eggs at his desk while managing a first round of emails before the
quiet would fill with a Skype call with Tommy Carter, his chief of
staff, and the arrival of a small, bustling crew that includes his wife,
Jean O. Saunders.

The orderly wall of accolades had his back. His Project Lifesaver
International uniform hung at the ready for the workday to
commence—as if, one fusing to the next by the solder of his ongoing
attention, any given workday ever actually ended.

He's a few good decades away but not much distance from
where he bolted out of the starting gate of this earthly go-round on
August 8, 1945, in Elizabeth City, North Carolina, and from where
he moved with his parents five years later: Norfolk, Virginia.

In those small East Coast harbor communities, young Jarvis Eugene Saunders Jr., informally known as "Gene," grew through Boy Scouts, sports and his parents' influence, to embrace the grit of life: challenge, teamwork, humanitarianism and personal responsibility.

Thinking back, he summed up childhood as a learning process—learning to take the good with the bad, the rewards with the consequences, the responsibilities with the roles and obligations.

"The sense of responsibility was probably the thing that was foremost with me," he recalled. "My parents instituted the belief that you stand up and take responsibility for what you do. You have the good and the bad; you misbehave and you pay for it," he explained. "If you were good, everything went fine. If you misbehaved, you knew you were going to pay for it. And you did."

The process had support in a time and place that lacked endorsement for the entitlement mindset. "And I don't see that I was psychologically scarred by it," Saunders affirmed. "You just learned. You learned that whatever you do has a consequence, be it good or bad."

During his formative years he thrived on activities, camaraderie and teamwork among others who understood that basic tenet and strove, as he did, for the sense of accomplishment and the recognition that result from going above and beyond within organizations devoted to a worthy common cause. He'd found his element and fit in well.

"You felt like you had a purpose, like what you were doing meant something to someone else and to you," he said.

These experiences reinforced the value of teamwork—of working with others and respecting that everybody plays a part, that no single person alone can accomplish it all.

Scouting offered mentoring, merit badges and introductions to leadership. The structured increments of personal development instilled enduring lessons of rewards and consequences and propelled his self-discovery of initiative, strengths and weaknesses, and leadership style.

"As you're in those kinds of organizations, and you progress through the ranks, they push you, from time to time, in leadership roles," Saunders explained. "And I think that's where you start to develop what leadership is. You may not understand it . . . but you start your learning phase of your style of leadership, and whether it's good, bad or indifferent, and what you have to do to get people to follow or assist you."

Astrologically speaking, he's as full-blooded a Leo as they come. Jean reminds him so.

"She says I fit the mold, whatever that is," Saunders mused, unsure of the charges. "If hard-headed is one of them, I'm pretty sure it's true."

Astrology writers put it more diplomatically, using such congenial descriptions as *strong personality* and *not shy about expressing oneself*. A sizeable list of enviable traits also pegs the astral lions as: bold, ambitious, courageous, intelligent; proud, passionate, protective of justice; natural trail-blazing leaders who embrace with gusto the challenges, the responsibilities and the glory of a worthy mission executed well.

Acronymically speaking, LEO comprises the industry initialism for *law-enforcement officer*. Purely incidental? Could be.

As for Saunders, once the seed of a deserving idea has taken root and begun to flourish in his mind, don't think for a second that telling him *you can't* will parch it. Withholding the flow of encouragement and moral or logistical provision won't starve the vine to wither. Conversely, the underestimation is sure to backfire, flipping inertia to the perdurance of ivy overcoming a castle wall— or perhaps a less delicate, more mammoth force.

"I was always bullheaded," Saunders proclaimed. "If I had something, and I felt really strongly about it, unless you could give me a really good, sensible reason *not* to do it," the pursuit ensued. "Don't give me this, 'Well, we've always done it this way, so that's good enough,'" he advised. "I didn't buy into that. I just *did not* buy into it."

At seventeen, primed for the path of service, Saunders joined the Virginia Army National Guard. Three days after high school graduation in 1963 he entered boot camp, kicking off a nearly fourteen-year National Guard career. By a fate he still can't fathom, he got to jump school, trained as a military paratrooper and was assigned to an engineer battalion as a communications crewman with the US Army's 101st Airborne Division.

Then Saunders attended National Guard Officer Candidate School and would proceed to fulfill the remainder of his commitment with infantry and military police units.

In August 1968, the month of his twenty-third birthday, Saunders joined the Chesapeake (Virginia) Police Department. The job met his expectations: rigorous training; responding to complaints, domestic disputes, criminal activity and non-criminal emergencies; arresting offenders when necessary. Nothing surprising; nothing intimidating; typical LEO terrain—coarse, craggy and demanding. But bureaucratically the decorum compared to that of a park: Stroll in line, don't get pushy and don't run around ruffling feathers.

The park is no place for a bullheaded lion.

NO GOOD MUZZLE FOR A RIGHTEOUS BELLOW

Chesapeake, Virginia, 1969/70

It wasn't the rookie's *beat* that depicted a park. At the close of a decade known for the national rise in recreational drug use that would usher then-President Richard Nixon's 1970 Controlled Substance Act and 1971 official declaration of America's War on Drugs, Saunders, a patrol officer, detected the increase of drug use and distribution on local streets—and more kids involved in the trade. He hated to see it. He knew the trajectory, understood the implications, and foresaw the impact that a rampant drug culture, if permitted to grow, would have on the citizens and their communities within his jurisdiction.

But within the department, others seemed to ignore the problem and its gravity, Saunders said. *That* was the park; *that's* where the inclination existed to take in the surface appearances and shallow depths of nature but overlook the swelling of an ugly, degenerative underbelly.

"We didn't have a narcotics squad," he recalled. He thought they should. He, for one, had become continuously privy to a battering ram of word-on-the-street intel that he could optimize, if not restrained by indifference. So just as a bullheaded lion won't be confined to a park, Saunders, in uniform and in his off-duty time, pursued nighttime drug busts in Chesapeake and worked as often as possible with nearby Norfolk PD's narcotics unit to hone his acumen. And just as the rising bellow of a bull cannot be restrained, nor would Saunders be muzzled by convention and politesse.

Back in Chesapeake, he continued to illuminate the drug problem internally: *It's happening, we need to deal with it now,* he recalled urging. Saunders knew that sooner or later they'd have to adapt. They would have to acknowledge the problem spilling out from the so-called big cities to permeate quiet small-town communities like his. If the department didn't address it, Chesapeake would fall behind the power curve.

He pushed to form a unit to specialize in narcotics—one for which getting drugs off the streets was the primary focus and by which cops were trained and equipped to handle the incidents effectively and get a proactive, preemptive grip on the threat. Typical patrol, vice and detective activities weren't adequate, "and if they did run into it, they didn't know what the hell to do with it," Saunders explained. "I felt like we needed to concentrate something on narcotics because it was getting bad." He also believed that the more prevalent the problem grew, the more that the media would expose it and likely admonish the department for not addressing it.

"Did they like it? No," Saunders supposed. "But I think in the back of their minds they saw *yeah, maybe this is really getting to the point we need to do something with it.*

"Well, apparently I ruffled feathers," Saunders continued. "In 1970 they started a narcotics unit, but they made sure I was not in it. Instead of putting me in narcotics, they put me in vice.

"I guess this was politics," the official cold shoulder, he opined. "They hadn't recognized the need, and I was being punished for bringing it to light."

Working vice, Saunders dispensed his valuable insights via drug-education talks to schools and organizations throughout the city. And, more distinctively, he began to amass critical intel that would lead not only to his transfer to the new narcotics squad, but also, deservedly, to spearheading one of the largest drug conspiracy cases in East Coast history at the time.

FOUR

Shake, Break, and Take 'em Down

"Well, how does it feel to have a career case?"
"What do you mean?"
"Guys go all their life and never have a case like this."
"Well, it was there, so I jumped on it."

Chesapeake, Virginia, 1970-73

"That was the Hubert Hoffler investigation," Saunders recalled. And it marked a defining departure from Chesapeake PD's beaten path.

While working vice, Saunders had gotten word of amphetamines and barbiturates being distributed as an organized effort, with ties to Chesapeake. "The guy who was running it was an old bootlegger. You know, graduated from whiskey to drugs," Saunders said. "And as I started really looking into this thing, I discovered that there was a fire captain who was involved with it, too."

The "old bootlegger" was Hubert E. Hoffler, a Chesapeake resident who, almost twenty years earlier, had been convicted with seven others of conspiracy to manufacture, remove and conceal distilled spirits in violation of the IRS laws.

But it was information that Saunders had been gleaning from users arrested by vice that led to Captain Maurice Griffin of the Chesapeake Fire Department.

"It was like a stair step," Saunders said. "You get information from this person, who leads you to that person, and to that person . . . and you just keep digging."

Saunders had sensed complexity and paid close attention to details that implied links between Griffin and Hoffler. He knew the men were friends, and he knew Hoffler's criminal background. Saunders made Griffin his primary target. And he'd have to be stealthy.

"We were not going to get him with an overt investigation—we were going to have to get him clandestine," Saunders recalled.

So he'd proposed a plan: Get a Norfolk police officer hired to the Chesapeake Fire Department, undercover, to gain inroads to Griffin and breach the secrecy protecting the ring.

"Mainly we wanted to put him in the station, working at the same time," Saunders recounted. "Once a comfort period passed, he would start making innuendoes that he wanted to get hold of some drugs to distribute, without directing comments to Griffin but letting him get the word.

"It took a little convincing," Saunders said of his pitch. "I've often been accused of having crazy ideas. Chesapeake was not a really sophisticated police department then. I was always told I was a step ahead; I was 'a big-city cop in a small-town police department,' according to the chief.

"The chief looked at me like I had three heads," Saunders mused. "Then he said, 'Well, if you think you can arrange it . . .' So I figured, *Okay, you gave me your blessing; I'm outta here!*"

It was 1971, and his scheme had scored a *go*. Saunders transferred to narcotics to execute it.

A few months into the operation, Griffin got receptive to "Charles," the undercover agent, and his quest for narcotics. He sold Charles a quantity of pills. Through multiple subsequent transactions involving hundreds more, Griffin had also gotten loose-lipped enough to dribble out where the stuff had originated and who played what roles along the import and distribution chain. He'd dropped names, including Hoffler, "the boss."

Saunders had already been onto Hoffler. And based on Charles' reports, which included names and phone calls between Griffin, Hoffler and others, he'd been expanding the investigation. But not everyone at the office shared his zeal.

"When we were looking at Hoffler, the enormity of what we were getting into actually bothered some of the people around me,"

Saunders recalled. "They felt like it was too big for us . . . a little bit too big for a local police department.

"Fortunately the chief didn't feel that way," he said. "And my feeling was, *The hell it is! Hoffler's in Chesapeake. He's doing business and it's being controlled from Chesapeake. We have not only a right, but a duty. We need to get in there and take care of this. And if we don't do it, it doesn't look good for us.*"

Hoffler lived in the Deep Creek section of Chesapeake, on George Washington Highway, a main thoroughfare. Saunders suspected he'd have enticed members of his former bootlegging network into this newer enterprise. Ongoing surveillance on Hoffler, his home and his guests added to a growing armory of evidence. Research into license plate registrants, links to other names, phone and bank records, criminal histories and more, tied up loose ends and helped flesh out the details revealing a sophisticated narcotics trafficking network led by the old bootlegger from his home in Saunders' territory.

The pills were being illegally concocted and packaged in Mexico. Traffickers smuggled 100,000 or more at a time hidden in hollowed-out compartments of automobile gas tanks from Ciudad Acuna, Mexico, across the Rio Grande into Del Rio, Texas, and east to Gainesville, Georgia. In Gainesville, batches got split up for distribution in different directions, much of it coming up the East Coast through South Carolina, North Carolina, Virginia and north. Cohorts included some of Hoffler's former bootlegging associates as well as truckers who comprised his original primary customer base.

US border patrol existed then, but "at that particular time, drug smuggling was far ahead of the law-enforcement response to it," Saunders said. "We were playing catch-up all the time. Every time you had what we called a 'mule,' he always had different ways of getting it across the border. And the gas tank was one of them.

"They had all kinds of tricks, and they still do," he said. "We're getting better at catching them, because we've learned the mules' tricks, but every time law-enforcement learns a trick, they come up with another one."

When he'd gathered enough evidence, Saunders sought arrests. He approached Chesapeake Commonwealth's Attorney Peter Axson.

"I said I not only wanted to take down Griffin, I want to take down the whole network, which at that time was considered a pretty huge undertaking—especially at the local level," Saunders said. "Now if you're talking *federal*, that's one thing. But here we're talking about a city police department that wants to take down an international drug ring.

"We went to Axson because we didn't want to get warrants," Saunders continued. "We wanted this case to go straight to the circuit court."

Pursuing warrants would lead them to general district court, where they would have had to lay out part of the case for a probable-cause hearing. Doing so could expose witnesses and informants. Alternatively, Axson could present probable cause to a grand jury, a confidential process, seeking indictments. If granted, police could obtain bench warrants from circuit court, make the arrests, "and then the *first* trial is *the* trial," Saunders explained. "That protects your evidence, and it protects your resources until the very last minute."

Around mid-1972, the grand jury issued indictments against Griffin, Hoffler and several others. Arrests ensued.

As expected, during interviews and interrogation some defendants gave up information and agreed to testify. "They wanted to make deals," Saunders said. And as a conspiracy case took shape, state and federal agencies would descend upon his local effort, something Saunders hadn't foreseen.

"The next thing I know," he continued, "I've got Virginia State Police knocking on my door; I have what was then the federal Bureau of Narcotics and Dangerous Drugs wanting to participate in interviews and carry the case out further," and "we'd already had some assistance from US Customs; they had gotten the 'mule' for us."

The agencies all had axes of their own to grind with Hoffler and associates.

More power to 'em.

As Saunders continued working up the case, the FBI's Norfolk office informed him that Hoffler had taken a contract on his life and that Saunders should protect himself. He moved his family to an undisclosed location.

"This guy Hoffler was a dangerous guy," Saunders said. One of the men arrested had stated that Hoffler wouldn't hesitate to do away with anyone he considered a potential threat to his operation or his pending defense. Known affiliates of Hoffler had been disappearing or turning up dead during the investigation.

"Of course at that time, because I was the chief investigator, I was a very big threat," Saunders said. Eliminating Saunders could slow the whole thing down enough for Hoffler to start working on witnesses, beginning with the signal that taking out the lead investigator would send to them. Hoffler didn't abide by the code that some other organized crime entities did, that you didn't go against law enforcement, Saunders explained. "His code was that he's going to do whatever it takes," no matter who gets hit. "If you crossed him in any way, you were subject to be eliminated.

"It pissed me off," Saunders continued. "I was determined at that point that this guy's going away. You know, I'm going to watch myself, but this guy's going away. He's just not going to get away with this. He's done too much, to too many people, for too long, and he's not gonna get away with it."

The threat to Saunders lasted about a month. But Saunders' threat to Hoffler had bigger teeth.

"We ended up convicting him," Saunders said. "Convicted all of them; every one of 'em."

Hoffler was convicted on drug conspiracy charges January 31, 1973 and sentenced to forty years. Griffin and the others followed in time.

That same year, US Customs had a case of their own to wrap. Saunders got a call from the Del Rio office asking him to identify a voice that agents had recorded from wiretaps. Sure enough: it was Hoffler. Saunders flew to Dallas to testify in a federal trial against his hometown's "old bootlegger" turned international drug lord.

According to Saunders, Hoffler turned out to be the biggest supplier of "reds" and "blacks" in the US at the time. He'd had a lock on pills on the East Coast and had been looking into expanding with cocaine and heroin.

As Saunders waited with customs agents in the hall outside the Dallas courtroom, US marshals escorted Hoffler past him.

"He looked at me, and you could tell he was surprised," Saunders recalled. "Not happy, and surprised.

"Well they go into the courtroom, and about fifteen or twenty minutes later they come out, then they're gone.

"So I'm asking, 'What happened?' The Customs guy said that Hubert Hoffler, as he walked in and saw me, changed his plea from not guilty to guilty." Unexpected but reassuring, Saunders said. "Once we had forty years on him in the penitentiary in Richmond, and then he was convicted of the federal charges, there was no way he was going to get out of jail for the rest of his life." With the exception of Hoffler's short stint as a prison escapee that summer, Saunders' assessment proved correct.

"It was an interesting time," Saunders said of the nearly three-year ordeal. "It was a big case, the first drug-conspiracy case of its kind ever in the Commonwealth of Virginia." And a worthy pursuit despite the resistance, he affirmed. "I guess during my career, I've ruffled a few feathers because of that tenacity, or that bullheadedness," he said. "But when you see things that need to be addressed, and you bring them to others' attention, and nothing happens, what's your alternative? Go into a corner, crawl up, cower and say *okay*?

"Or do you go out and do something about it?"

Saunders admits he didn't always know exactly how to handle a situation, other than "the only way I knew at that time," he said. "I wasn't a very good politician," he noted. "I guess I've been one of those *Damn the torpedoes, full speed ahead!* guys," but eventually things worked out.

After all these years, amid all the down-and-dirty events of that long, drawn-out battle, one brief commentary from a fellow LEO still makes Saunders grin.

"The BNDD guy comes up and says, 'Well how does it feel to have a career case?'

"I said, 'What do you mean?'

"He says, 'Guys go all their life and never have a case like this.'

"I didn't pay much attention to that because, you know, I'm a local cop. What am I going to get for doing this? I got satisfaction that we took down an international drug ring.

"So I said, 'Well, it was there, so I jumped on it.'"

THE PERSISTENT HOOK OF A GOOD CONSPIRACY; 1973 AND LATER

"I loved working conspiracies. I was into it," Saunders said, laughing. They kept his mind constantly in gear, as much off-duty as on, connecting dots. "It was always a challenge," he explained. "And you're always thinking about it: *How do I tie this to that? How can I prove this? Where do I think this will lead? Is this person tied to this person, and if they are tied, how do I prove it?*" Like a jigsaw puzzle only better, he noted. "I don't do jigsaw puzzles," he said, laughing at his limits for sedentary activities; "I don't have the patience. But a conspiracy? That was different. I'm on the run, I'm moving, I'm doing."

Results-wise, "conspiracies were the way to go," Saunders continued. "You could wrap up the whole organization, not just one guy. You have to be a little more patient—you take down one; you develop information. You tie all the ends together; you substantiate the information. As you got information on the next level, you had to put all that together so that you could *prove* that next level. Then you just start taking them down in bunches. Because if you take down four or five people, you can bet that one of them is going to tell you something more.

"It's a good result," Saunders said. "Not only do you take down the bad guys, but you shut down that organization. You're taking the underpinnings out, so they cease to function.

"And any law-enforcement officer will tell you there's a sense of inner satisfaction when you're able to do this and it turns out successful," he declared. "You're working for your own sense of that because you're not going to get a lot of accolades. What you're doing, you're doing for other reasons. For one, you're pitting yourself against 'them.' It's almost like a hunt. It's kind of hard to describe, but there's that inner drive: *I'm gonna do this, I'm gonna take this guy down, and I'm gonna take down everybody around him. I'm not going to be satisfied with just him.*"

Saunders recalled two other large-scale conspiracy cases under his charge in that era.

In 1973, following the Hoffler wrap-up, he had transferred from narcotics to the felony squad. There he uncovered another East Coast organized-crime ring, this one operating between Chesapeake and Buffalo, New York.

"We got a uniform call," Saunders recalled. "A guy had bought a TV and felt like there was something wrong with the transaction. So I went in, talked to him, looked at the TV, started running the serial numbers, and found out the TV was out of the General Electric warehouse in Chesapeake."

Warehouse workers in Chesapeake and truck drivers from Buffalo had been onboarding unauthorized appliances and other merchandise for transport to people who then sold the stolen goods from their cars. Saunders recalled his investigation nabbing about four people before that case fell to the feds.

1980 marked the takedown of an international cocaine-trafficking ring headquartered in North Carolina and set up for distribution in Chesapeake. Then-Sergeant Saunders led the investigation, dubbed Operation Snow Cat, which evolved into a joint taskforce including Norfolk and Virginia state police. To Saunders' dismay, this ring involved a firefighter just as Hoffler's had, and worse: As he took down little guys within the organization and climbed the ladder to its "bigger fish," Saunders discovered several law-enforcement officers in conspiratorial cahoots—some of whom had been working with him on that very case.

The breach of trust and dishonorable behavior struck him as "very sobering," Saunders recalled. "It was shocking, it was surprising, but you had to get over it," he said. "You had to move on."

It also introduced him to the special brand of betrayal that he would meet again, decades later, within trusted circles of staff and partners at Project Lifesaver.

FIVE

Fighting the Old Regime

"I was hard-headed. And they were not going to push me out of the way. I was going to fight it all the way."

—*Chief Gene Saunders*

By 1973, Saunders had been involved in too many barricade situations and other incidents that had ended badly due to what he described as *undisciplined response*. Had they been handled by a trained, disciplined tactical team rather than "a potpourri of cops" with nobody in charge and everybody doing his own thing, they'd likely have resolved successfully, he said.

He had noted the impact of Special Weapons and Tactics, or SWAT, units that had been cropping up around the country for almost a decade in response to a rise in more sophisticated, coordinated, or otherwise extraordinary criminal events and special operations. The SWATs were select-focus paramilitary police units that had branched away from the world of ordinary law-enforcement duties and into the realm of extra-high-risk mission-oriented team deployments—right up Saunders' alley.

SWAT made sense to Saunders, and he petitioned the Chesapeake PD to establish a unit. Not yet a sergeant himself, Saunders urged his superiors to heed his cautions and observations and not to believe that any situation happening elsewhere couldn't happen in Chesapeake, "because it can, and it will," he'd repeatedly warned. He'd proven so with his push for a narcotics unit and the subsequent takedown of hometown-Hoffler's international drug ring. The intuition, tenacity and results that he'd demonstrated for more than three years should have spoken volumes for the credibility and integrity of his visionary and leadership prowess moving forward.

But the brush-off prevailed: *Oh, this is Chesapeake; it won't happen here.*

Bull crap, Saunders thought. And he pressed, prodded and played the politics to further departmental evolution.

Eventually his deputy chief yielded to the idea and assigned four sergeants to develop it—to the exclusion of a leadership role for Saunders, its prime protagonist.

But one man's hammer of discouragement need not forge another man's chains of restraint.

"I was hard-headed," Saunders recalled. "And they were not going to push me out of the way. I was going to fight it all the way."

In another excursion from the bureaucratic park—and somebody should have seen it coming—Saunders took it upon himself to lay out an organizational chart for establishing the new unit.

"I went to the guy who was senior to me, the sergeant, and I gave it to him," he recalled. The sergeant showed the plans to the deputy chief, who commended him on a great job, Saunders said, and then the sergeant credited Saunders, thus setting the record straight. Finally Saunders, undeniably qualified, was assigned to help co-found the unit. He took the lead in establishing training, credentials, certifications and operational procedures, and soon thereafter inherited the role of commander.

Initially, despite its asset potential, SWAT was a hard sell within the department in terms of the trust and rapid integration it deserved, Saunders said.

"The whole time SWAT was developing, we had to fight the old regime: *This has been this way for twenty years; it's still the way it should be*," he recalled of fixed thinking and static protocol. "Well, it wasn't," he lamented. "Things had changed." Criminals had new activities, and they were becoming meaner and more aggressive, he explained. "You couldn't handle it the way you did before. There would be incidents where SWAT should have been called and they weren't. And the incidents did not always end well."

According to Saunders, and just as he had feared, it took a police officer being killed in a barricade situation before SWAT became the default for such special-focus incidents.

"I knew that was going to happen," he said. "I knew that's the way it was going to develop, and I had not wanted it to."

Mid-decade, Saunders had to choose between his commitment to the police department and that to the National Guard, two once-complementary arms of service whose demands on Saunders had grown incompatible. To stay with the Guard, he'd have to be free to participate in Guard drills and to answer the call to active duty, which, in his day, could cost a police officer his job. Furthermore, in addition to leading SWAT, Saunders had been working undercover with the police department's narcotics squad. Maintaining a clean-cut military appearance could have blown his cover to astute criminals.

After fourteen years with National Guard, Saunders resigned from service and remained on the police force. There he would continue to lead its SWAT unit for the remainder of his total twenty-three years as commander, through more than 800 successful operations ranging from search and rescue, hostage rescue and barricaded subjects to high-risk raids and sniper showdowns. And new doors opened all the while as he trained, consulted and worked with SWAT teams in other states.

"It was during that time that I was able to establish some tremendous military liaisons," he recalled. Those led to professional-enrichment experiences with the United States Army and Navy not normally available to police officers. Saunders and members of his team trained with the Navy's Underwater Demolition Teams, Army Special Forces and Navy Explosive Ordnance Disposal technicians, and trained and worked with Naval Special Warfare SEALs. Saunders also completed Marine Amphibious Reconnaissance School, Army Ranger School and several Naval Special Warfare training courses.

To discover or create such opportunities, "you really have to dig deep and get good relationships, which I was very fortunate to be able to do," he recalled.

Some of those relationships have sustained through the decades, and several he established while training with SEAL Team Six during the 1990s. Capt. Ronald Yeaw, then the team's commanding officer, recalled Saunders approaching him around 1991: "He wanted to know if I was willing to offer up some of my shooters to help him build and train his SWAT team," Yeaw said during an interview in 2018. "So I said, 'Absolutely, no problem.'" In the years that followed, members of SEAL Team Six's Blue Team helped Saunders strengthen what Yeaw described as "a very credible and well-trained SWAT team."

One of those SEALs was Scott Howerton. Howerton, who is now retired and volunteers for PLI, trained and observed Saunders and his agents several times a year from 1993 until his own 2000 deployment to Bahrain. As a leader, "he was very good; very decisive; very to the point," Howerton recalled of Saunders. "Basically it was lessons learned," he said, explaining that no matter how hard or how rewarding they were, "the lessons learned, he utilizes those and puts them into action."

The ongoing cross-training between military and law-enforcement fields back then kept Saunders sharp, connected and forward-acting—critical qualities for continuous development in visionary and effective leaders.

And he continued one of his favorite pastimes: parachuting. Despite the lure of the freefall to other presumed adrenaline junkies, that wasn't what delivered the fix to Saunders.

"I used to open high—in other words, *deploy high*," he said. "Because I love the peace and serenity of coming down, of just being able to listen to the wind ripple through the parachute and just see the scenery.

"And it's quiet," he concluded. "You know, you get a couple of minutes of just the most peaceful serenity that you can find."

Ironically, it's also the scariest thing he's ever done . . . and done again . . . and again . . ..

SLASHING THE WEEDS SURROUNDING
A PERENNIAL CHALLENGE

> *"Don't stay on the paths, because they're not going to. If all
> you're going to do is walk down a path, you're not going to
> accomplish anything. You gotta get out there and break
> the bush. You gotta get into the rough area."*

—*Chief Gene Saunders*

With the development of SWAT came a logical increase in reliance
upon the agents' mission mentality and special-focus expertise
for search-and-rescue assignments. In time, all search-and-rescue
operations funneled to SWAT.

Saunders recalled one assignment, in the late 1980s, when
a woman in her eighties had wandered from home. Alzheimer's
disease had rendered her helpless on her own. Saunders helped
coordinate the search, but with his own wife in the hospital he turned
the mission over to his second in command. The team searched for
two days with no luck. Eventually the woman was found in a creek,
deceased, only about 50 yards outside the search area, he recalled.

"Those are the kinds of things that you think, *geez, 50 yards. If
we had only enlarged our search,*" he said. "Those are the kinds of
things that bother me."

In another incident, searchers found a missing man alive, in a
doghouse, after seven hours.

In a third, a man had walked away from an assisted-living home.
"When rescuers initially went out there, they didn't really do a *search*
search," Saunders recalled. "They just kind of rode around and
looked." He sent the team back to "cover every inch" surrounding
the point of origin. "And as we're searching," he said, "I get a call
from one of the SWAT guys. About 100 yards from the assisted-
living home he was walking in ankle-deep brush, he stepped down
into a culvert, and he stepped on the guy.

"*Stepped* on him!

"He was covered with foliage," Saunders continued. "And when
the searcher stepped on him, the guy hollered. So we found him. And

the only reason we found him was because we went back and said, *I don't like the way this area was covered; we're gonna do it again.*"

A search for another elderly woman lasted about two weeks with no success. Months later, two horseback riders found her body in a ditch. "She wasn't 50 yards away from the nursing home," Saunders said. "I think that's the one that drove it home for me: Always cover the area completely within about a quarter of a mile of that area where they were last seen."

And of course, there had been the failure in '89, in Western Branch, the spawn of which had been growing claws as it festered in Saunders' hallowed private space.

THE PRICE OF PERSISTENCE

A good search required considerable resources. A typical event on Saunders' watch averaged approximately eight to ten hours, at a cost of $1,500 per hour, and some fifty to 100 people, including about thirty-five SWAT members and ten to fifteen patrol officers. And while access to this manpower is critical, managing it has its own challenges.

People get tired. It's hard work to hike rough grounds and plow bodily through thick vegetation, Saunders explained. And when people get tired, they get distracted. "It's a human reaction," he noted, "and there's nothing you can do to stop it. Sure, the better shape somebody's in, the longer they will last," he affirmed, but at some point even they succumb as their physical endurance outlasts their attentiveness, he said. "So you have to constantly be thinking about relieving people.

"So many things are going on," Saunders continued. "It's a multitude of things. And you're dealing with the family, and you're dealing with your boss; you're dealing with the press and everybody else in the world who wants to know what's going on. You're getting calls from Virginia Department of Emergency Management: 'Do you need more resources?' Well, I can always use more resources," he said, "but sometimes the more resources you get in, the harder it is to manage them.

"It can get to be a real bear."

What's worst? The know-it-alls. "You get more criticism from people who have absolutely no idea what it's all about than anybody else," Saunders said. "It's not enough that you're doing it to yourself; now you've got all the armchair quarterbacks, and your bosses," judging a situation from afar. "'Why didn't you do *this*, why didn't you do *that*, why didn't you do the *other*?'" he echoed. "'Did you do *this*? Did you do *that*? . . .' and most of them we did," he said. "Did we always do them at the right time? I don't know." Sure, others can *talk* all about it, but what do they *know* about it if they haven't been in the trenches?

"And you see it in the news today with police work," Saunders said. "You know, everybody watches television and wonders why the police didn't solve some homicide in an hour like they did on *Law and Order*. You have all these people who have no clue what it's like to do the job, have never done it in their life, and watch something on TV and think they are experts on it. And the next thing you know, you're having to stand and answer their questions."

Furthermore, public perception didn't align with reality. Throughout the mid-1970s to early 1990s, more of the department's searches than not involved Alzheimer's patients. And this uniquely impaired population could no more effectively help rescuers than they could help themselves.

"When you searched for them, it wasn't like you were searching for a 'normally' cognitive person who could help themselves, and maybe leave clues, and if you called out their name they would answer," Saunders explained. "Because Alzheimer's patients, I quickly learned, wouldn't answer you." They simply cannot assist in their own cause without the necessary cognitive awareness, judgement and communicative wherewithal.

"So you talk to the family: 'Has he done this before?' 'Where did he go?'" Saunders said. "And while that sometimes brings success, sometimes it doesn't. Because they may go to the same place four times, and the fifth time they don't go that way. They go a completely different way.

"And this is one of the things that I kept telling people all the time in searches," he concluded: "Don't stay on the paths, because they're not going to. If all you're going to do is walk down a path, you're not going to accomplish anything. You gotta get out there and break the bush. You gotta get into the rough area."

While research on Alzheimer's disease ramped up in the 1970s, and in 1976, according to the Alzheimer's Association, the affliction had been officially declared "the most common form of dementia and a major public health challenge" by neurologist Robert Katzman in his editorial published in *Archives of Neurology*, it would still be years before awareness about the disease and its effects would be widespread for public and public-safety consumption, and even longer before special danger-prevention strategies and search protocols would be developed. To that latter end, Saunders would become a pioneer of sorts.

SIX

Deploying Grit

*What the lost were thinking when they left their points of origin;
where they thought they were headed and why; how
they would be able to navigate . . . all of it was
anybody's scientific, wild-ass guess.*

hree years and numerous searches—many successful, others
not—had passed since that death in Chesapeake's Western
Branch that defined the spawning of Saunders' internal beast.
Saunders was still entrenched in search and rescue as commander
of the police department's SWAT unit, and he'd been volunteering
elsewhere for the cause as well, when in 1992 he approached Sheriff
John Newhart to embed an already-intact voluntary search-and-
rescue auxiliary at the Chesapeake Sheriff's Office. It was composed
of ardent members of various Ranger, aviation and infantry units, US
military Special Forces, and several special-operations communities.

Saunders had been entrenched with the staunchest devotees
for years, having commanded, led, taught and/or worked alongside
them in organizations such as the Virginia State Militia, Virginia
Defense Force, The Lafayette Brigade and the US Air Force Auxiliary,
also known as the Civil Air Patrol.

The corps had stuck together as a cohesive Ranger-style
operational group based within such organizations. They had
a serious search-and-rescue history as the die-hards known to
cover the toughest terrains, the worst environments, the hairiest

"swamp-up-to-the-neck" conditions. Grit was their forte. But the unit had grown dissatisfied with the sense of undervaluation by the affiliates hosting them. According to Saunders, their "hard-charging Army Ranger attitude" wasn't always appreciated by more laid-back organizations' personnel who "didn't know how to deal with that kind of psyche," he said, laughing. His team had recently been displaced, and Saunders intended to sustain its morale, its impact and its exceptional virtue.

Sheriff Newhart embraced the unit with all its repute and fortitude. The team became the 43rd Virginia Search and Rescue, a name evolved from Civil War Ranger heritage and Commander John Singleton Mosby's 43rd Battalion, Virginia Cavalry, also known as Mosby's Rangers. Saunders led as chief.

This facilitated a subsequent, logical channeling of search missions from Saunders' SWAT unit, which needed relief in the face of escalating overall demand, to his new and eager 43rd Virginia Search and Rescue at Chesapeake Sheriff's Office.

Just as Saunders and his search teams with police, civilian and military forces had observed for years, incidents involving Alzheimer's patients continued to prevail. Yet the available education and resources pertaining to the inherent challenges seemed inadequate, if not nonexistent.

He and his teams understood that people afflicted with Alzheimer's disease—and other intellectual impairments, for that matter—hadn't the cognitive faculties to help themselves or those trying to find or assist them. What the lost were thinking when they left their points of origin; where they thought they were headed and why; how they would be able to navigate and manage the terrains, the temperatures, the nightfalls, the traffic, the human and animal interactions and other variables along the way—all of it was anybody's guess. Anybody's scientific, wild-ass guess.

Who can extract rhyme or reason from what ensues of the discord in a faraway mind?

And how could a man who devoted nearly every waking hour to protecting others not spend much of his time perplexed and unsettled by best attempts rendered futile and failures he'd never deemed an option?

"When you get to a point when you're not finding them, or you're finding them too late," Saunders said of those haunting conclusions, "you can't help but probe, *how can we do this better? How can we get out there and find these people?*"

SEVEN

A Birdseye Review

*"I loved SWAT. Loved every minute of it. I just wanted to
lead a group of people who were highly trained, very effective
all committed to the same goal and willing to put in
what was necessary to achieve that."*

—*Chief Gene Saunders*

I n 2017 and 2018, Saunders reflected on some of the uncommon experiences, demands and effects of his police career. As he reminisced, nostalgia erased thirty years from his appearance.

"I think that sometimes maybe I wasn't as politically correct as I should have been," Saunders said, "but then I think that if I had been politically correct, nothing would have happened. Because, did I piss people off by doing that? Well, I sure did," he admitted. "Guys at the top? Oh, yeah. Oh, yeah." He laughed. "Because I think some of them were embarrassed," he said. For instance, "here this lone cop out there is showing them that there's a narcotics problem in our city, and we didn't do anything about it, and we didn't recognize it. Well, it's not like I snuck it up on 'em," Saunders said of his ongoing warnings. "I told them.

"And then with the SWAT team," he continued, "I felt like there was a very big need for it. I got fought in every direction. But I kept being that little mosquito whizzing around their heads. So finally, they let us create it."

Battle by battle, Saunders made inroads across a field both

needy and primed for modernization. "And then," he recalled, "all of a sudden, it just kind of came to me to create things."

His subsequent initiatives included founding the department's Citizens' Police Academy, which in 2018 was still going strong, and handicapped-parking enforcement in advocacy of the citizens for whom the designated parking spaces were designed.

Saunders also requested permission to install paramedics on the SWAT team. "Big battle there," he recalled. "I had people in the police department who said 'No, we don't need any firemen working with the police.' I said, 'Why not? I think we need to have paramedics with SWAT. The things we do are inherently dangerous, and I think it would behoove us to have medical people right there.'" And once Saunders got the OK for that, he also recruited a team physician who accompanied the team on operations.

Eventually most of his "crazy" ideas turned standard operating procedure for the department. There he had created channels for the sense of purpose, mission, leadership and teamwork that so comprised his own nature. Each success affirmed and encouraged his intuition, vision, and organizational competence while simultaneously serving a calling far more profound than personal gratification.

His initiatives often represented greater responsibility than others wittingly sought, but he hadn't thought about it in that light. "I loved SWAT," Saunders said, brimming. "Loved every minute of it. And I loved narcotics. I just wanted to lead a group of people who were highly trained, very effective, all committed to the same goal and willing to put in what was necessary to achieve that," he said. The job ushered in challenge, personal development and his ability to facilitate that course for kindred spirits, and ultimately to build something that would improve his corner of the world.

Of the extra training and activities shot to his inner adrenaline junkie, "I think the most satisfaction, the best time I ever had, was when I was embedded with the SEALs," Saunders said. What a rush. "I loved every second of that. Every second. It beat the hell out of me," he admitted, laughing, "and I loved every minute of it."

The best thing about a rush of that kind is its persistence: how it builds in the blood; how it lingers in the cells; how the moral satisfaction remains long after delivery of the fix. It's a natural high released by the continuous drip of rare chemistry.

"Being accepted by them was probably one of the biggest highlights of my life," Saunders said on a reverent note. "You know, here you are with guys who are known as the elite of the elite," he said. "First off, how many guys get that opportunity?" he posed. The awe-inspiring quality of the character, training and extreme fortitude that he and his agents experienced while entrenched with SEAL Team Six would still be understated, even when declared the total game-changer that it was.

"And they have such a close brotherhood," he said of the team's impermeable bond. But while the bond couldn't be broken from the outside, it could, when warranted, be shared and enhanced from within. "The day that they accepted me in," Saunders recalled of his ceremonial induction, "they gave me a patch, and they gave me a certificate and gave me a Trident . . . I was an honorary SEAL."

That event spoke volumes, he said, rhapsodizing, "How many guys do these particular kinds of guys let into the inner sanctum?" The acknowledgement transcended what could ever be expressed with words alone. "They paid me the ultimate compliment," Saunders said. "They absolutely did. I couldn't have asked for anything more." He searched for a moment, then concluded: "You can't do better than that. You just can't do better than that."

PSYCHIC DIVES

As for the job itself, "it has its good and its bad," the quintessential LEO broached. "It's a double-edged sword. . . .

"For one thing, it's taught me to be much more aware of my surroundings, what we call *situational awareness*," he said.

Civilians tag it *hypervigilance*. In Saunders' case, it's a heightened and automatic observation of and attention to the people, sounds and activities surrounding him in stores, restaurants and other public places, and cops develop it quickly. Call it profiling if you must, but omit the unwarranted tone of derogation. "If they've been in law-enforcement long enough, every person cops see or come across, they're analyzing," Saunders asserted. "And not in a negative way, but just paying close attention," he explained.

Even today, the details clamor: Who and what's behind him? What was that out-of-place noise? Who's entering or leaving the premises, and how are they behaving? It's rational; it's appropriate; it was required for the dangerous job entrusted to any public-safety servant. "As long as they're within my scope of attention, I'm gonna notice them," Saunders said unapologetically. "I'm going to notice things about them." And it could be the way somebody says something, or a person's body language, or the situation itself, that triggers an intuitive, sometimes visceral, alert, he added, presenting a slightly exaggerated but not-uncommon scenario: "You're walking down a dark street at night, and all of a sudden the hair on the back of your neck stands up," he suggested. "Well, you pay attention to that. What's caused that?"

While this sensory acuteness adds value to an officer's personal—professional toolset—and enhances his or her marketability, as evidenced in how cops become sought-after for safety and security work in their off-duty or retirement time—a nearly continuous state of elevated alertness takes a toll on the human mind and body. And these days cops face more stress with increased threats to their own safety, Saunders said, citing the sick and sickening rise in anti-cop violence in recent years. In response to that, "we're having to redefine threatening situations," he said. And that's a fact and a process that's apparently still lost on a public inclined to forgo critical thinking for the spoon-feeding of biased media commentary and the exploitive narratives crafted by political hijackers of serious societal problems.

During his own career, Saunders' situational awareness, gut-level instinctiveness and threat-assessment abilities matured with the military training he received in his SWAT years. Moreover, he recalled an unexpected, and still appreciated, word of acknowledgement by one of the military men back then: "I know this might sound crass," Saunders said, "but he said, 'You know, we know what we're going into when we do it. We get a mission; we know what we're in for. But you guys walk into it every day, every minute, and never know.'"

An astute point; and the man was correct, Saunders noted. "From minute to minute, you don't know what's going to happen on duty," he said. "You can be walking into a combat situation and never have any idea." He often considers the implications of that.

"I think cops are getting PTSD," Saunders posited.

Appropriately, much awareness has been raised about the effects of post-traumatic stress disorder on abuse victims and military combat veterans who've witnessed and/or experienced physical, mental and psychological trauma. Yet its effects on police officers might still be underestimated, Saunders said.

"You spend fifteen, twenty, twenty-five or thirty years in high-risk situations, never knowing when they're going to happen, rolling into things and having to be keenly aware all the time; and seeing what people can do to each other, and then being put into situations where your life is on the line," he explained. Any given day can present several hours of complete boredom and then twenty-five minutes of the most intense fear, terror and anxiety one can face, Saunders submitted. "So what happens to you when that goes on, that adrenaline rush every day—sometimes once a day, sometimes five times a day, sometimes eight times a day; sometimes for twenty minutes, sometimes for eight, nine, ten or twelve hours in a SWAT situation?"

It's a chemical roller coaster. It's a pervasive air of random provocation blowing through the fight-or-flight amusement park.

"Cops do it every day," Saunders said. No wonder they're always on edge. "It has an effect," he asserted. "Do I think they're getting PTSD? Yes, I do. Do they recognize it? Probably not."

If he could bust a few myths about police officers, those would include public misconceptions shaped by these occupational reflexes. But one leads the rest by far: Civilians tend to perceive cops as not having feelings, Saunders said. "Well, it's not that they don't have any feelings," he countered. "They've got a job to do, and they can't let the feelings get in the way," he explained.

Even Jean Saunders wonders how her husband ever dealt with the real-life horrors that she only sees on the screen: violent crime, violent accidents, behavior so gruesome and inhumane that it actually *does* become the inspiration and conceptual direction for the nearly unimaginable psychological thrillers that the rest of us watch from the safety of living rooms and movie theaters, and may struggle for days to purge from our senses.

How does a person's heart and mind reconcile the dissonance between the two intrinsically conflicted realities where he is obligated to operate? How does he discern with confidence which values he can effectively and justifiably carry from one reality paradigm to another? How does he settle up with a well-meaning conscience that calls his moral integrity out and whips him with accusations of *compromise* or *failure*?

Cops have no choice but to figure it out. "You just kind of separate it," put it out of mind, Saunders said of the perplexities. "The one thing I learned in the job is to always keep your personal feelings and your professional feelings apart," he noted. It's not necessarily easy, or even ideal, but "you have to," he asserted, "because it plays on you too much.

"It's like, you're in a SWAT situation, a hostage situation or something," he continued. "You just walk in with the attitude that you're going to handle it. And you go hours and hours and hours dealing with it. . . . You gotta be careful," he warned. "You're inclined to personalize it, but you know better.

"So you turn off that switch," he said. "You suppress certain feelings and emotions because you have to. You know, you deal with the incident as a thing you have to do. You get it done, and you walk away from it. And suppress it.

"And at the end of the day, after you've dealt with this, what do you do? Well, you go back and you debrief, you talk about it, 'What could we have done better?' and all this kind of stuff—and we always did that on search-and-rescue missions. Then you walk away from it, and it's like, OK, you just wipe it out," he said. "You don't think about it anymore. You try to turn it off.

"Well," Saunders continued, wincing, "you may not think about it anymore. But I don't think you *really* wipe it out. I don't think it goes away. It's still there," he said. "And if you hit the right key, it's gonna come back up."

The search-and-rescue defeats had always weighed too heavily on Saunders. Perhaps the lack of a bad-guy element in search situations created a vacuum in the adrenaline rush to be filled, instead, with empathy. It was hard to separate the job from the man, the professional from the personal. And without warning, the empathy could disable his "off" switch.

Instinctively, he knew better than to suppress these feelings. "You turn it off for so long," Saunders said, and the dormancy strengthens the beast. "Then it starts coming back to you."

What's more, shutdown prevents resolution.

Something about feeling his way through those losses would just have to claim its place. And in allowing that, Saunders had been honoring some quiet inner drive, paving and prepping a road to success that he had yet to even envision.

SWAT team, 1992

Saunders in police uniform

Extreme Makeover set just outside of Detroit. Early 2000s

First PLI Headquarters, trailer at Chesapeake Municipal Airport, 2000

Sheriff Newhart, Saunders, and Benny Rogerson
receiving the Alzheimer's Stand by Us Award, 2001

Virginia Beach helicopter flight officer, 2002

Chief with Pilot International ladies after receiving Virginia Best Practice
Award for Seniors programs, Chesapeake, 2013

Receiving a grant for
$98,000 from Suzanne
Wright, Autism Speaks
Founder, for transmitters for
Autistic children, 2015

Receiving Person of Distinction Award on Capitol Hill, 2016

Training the Live Oak Florida Police Department, 2016

Saunders, Ken Young (Lockheed Martin) and Tommy Carter
with PLI Indago drone, 2016

UAV instructor training in Chesapeake, Gary Reynolds in control, 2017

Saunders and Tommy Carter speaking at Indian River
County Sheriff's Citizen's Academy, 2017

Saunders, Jean and Sheriff Mascara at press conference for
St. Lucie County, Florida's start of program, 2018

Orange County press conference, 2018

Saunders speaking at Alzheimers's Foundation— PLI conference in Fairfax, Virginia, 2018

LA County training, 2018

LA County training, 2018

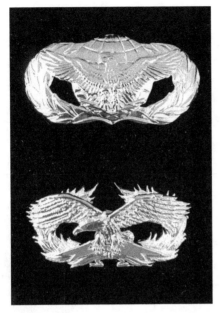

Electronic Search
Specialist badges
(top to bottom) basic
qualification and master
qualification

Saunders with his
inspiration, Jean

Tommy Carter and Gene Saunders in London

The gang doing the NASDAQ closing bell

Virginia Beach Police helo flying over Cape Henry Lighthouse

Saunders in awards dress uniform at his office

Promo picture for
autism rescue

Saunders with his
buddy Campbell

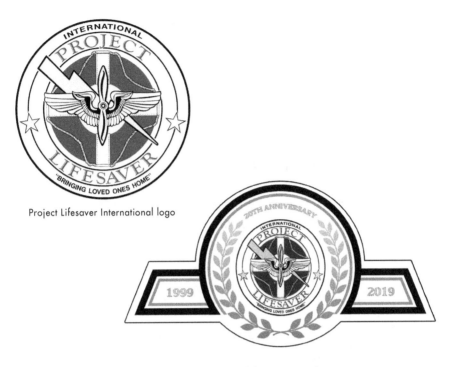

Project Lifesaver International logo

20th anniversary logo

Chesapeake office, RF Operations and Training

EIGHT

A Counter-Antagonist

*"Now Sheriff, . . . You need to understand
that once we start this, we can't stop it."*

Quelling inner torment ain't easy. Some sedate it, some souse it, some fight it ceaselessly with everything they've got.

It's the ultimate personal nemesis, yet we host it with all our hearts. But those who respect its power, challenge its inroads, and master the art and irony of such dubious hospitality can put a beast to bed for others.

"I think the saving grace for me has been Project Lifesaver," Saunders said. "Now, I'm channeling everything in a whole different direction that is far less negative."

Chesapeake, Virginia, late 1990s

Saunders had been in charge of both SWAT and the 43rd Virginia Search and Rescue until 1996, when he retired from SWAT. He remained chief of the 43rd at the sheriff's office and captain at Chesapeake PD, and in 1997 he began a four- to five-year stint as a volunteer flight officer with the Virginia Beach Police Department, where he learned to fly helicopters.

Inspiration reigned in summer 1998, following Sheriff Newhart's return from a National Sheriffs' Association conference. Newhart had collected information on electronic equipment being used to track wildlife. He shared it with his undersheriff, Col. David Newby. Newby thought it might interest Saunders. He was right.

Upon review of the materials, Saunders pondered the lifesaving potential. If wildlife could be tracked, why not people? He began to envision a new, proactive rather than reactive, approach to controlling the perennial nightmare starring some of the most vulnerable members of his own community: those with dementia and other cognitive impairments at risk of straying from safety toward catastrophe.

All the dots were connecting now, outlining a new, multifaceted tragedy-mitigation plan for finding people quickly and returning them alive to family and caretakers. Such an enhanced search-and-rescue program would include this crucial element that Saunders wondered why he hadn't ever seen employed: technology that search teams could use to track personal radio-frequency signals emitted passively by participants who had been reported missing. Simple but brilliant. Individual participants wearing transmitters could be found by searchers using receivers tuned to the appropriate designated radio frequency.

Saunders considered the lives they could save, not to mention the excessive time, money and other resources typically spent on routine missions—successful or not. The average standard search could take nine hours and cost $13,500 and ultimately still not deliver the human ROI.

Ideas and implications flooded Saunders' mind. He began researching the equipment. A conceptual search-and-rescue overhaul ensued as new information offered hope for exhausted methodology. Applying decades' worth of knowledge and experience, he began ticking boxes, known challenges, that might now be overcome. The only facet absent from his expanding vision was a good-enough reason *not* to heed it. The switch was "on," and Saunders had a beast to revisit.

He rolled out his vision to Benny Rogerson, a captain with the Norfolk PD and Saunders' executive officer at the 43rd Virginia Search and Rescue. The men knocked it around, framed scenarios, kicked its proverbial tires, probed for holes.

By preliminary analysis the machine looked sound—dare they consider *game-changing*?

Further inquiry into the equipment led to the discovery of a group in North Carolina that had begun using it for search in a limited fashion, and they had reported some success. Saunders met with the group to assess their approach. He came away unimpressed by their particular model and use of the technology, but the up-close look affirmed the possibilities for optimization inherent in the more sophisticated, complex plan he had been drafting.

For starters, Saunders hoped to establish and equip Chesapeake Sheriff's Office deputies and the 43rd Virginia Search and Rescue team collectively as the responding unit.

He contacted the equipment manufacturer. Ongoing correspondence evolved into strategy sessions and bore the insights that Saunders and Rogerson needed to reassess the feasibility of Saunders' plan.

They reframed scenarios, calibrated efficiencies, ran all the numbers.

Still sound. Increasingly compelling. Surpassing *feasible* for *absolutely necessary*.

What a project. A purposeful, promising, *life-saving project*.

Undersheriff Newby agreed, and, when approached with a proposal and fairly fleshed-out plan for training and search procedure, Sheriff Newhart approved.

Saunders' theory had passed muster, but "theories don't go anywhere without money," he recalled of his next challenge.

He purchased enough equipment with funds from the 43rd's treasury to begin team training, and shortly thereafter, a member of the North Carolina group delivered rudimentary tutelage regarding equipment functionality, bracelet fitting and signal tracking.

The tracking process involved a member of the search team doing a "360 swing," or a 360-degree spin, with a receiver tuned to the frequency of the bracelet, attempting to get a signal. On land, a signal could be detected from a mile or more away, depending upon the weather and terrain. Once the agent began getting signals, he or she then narrowed down to the strongest one and followed that direction. Audible chirps and a meter helped guide the agent further along the path toward the transmitting device. As the agent got closer to the client, the client's unique ID appeared on the agent's receiving screen.

For the occasions when they couldn't get a signal immediately, Saunders and his team developed their own methods, including alternative, complementary patterns of search, and installing an antenna atop a car to increase the signal range and the speed of area coverage.

Things were looking good. Saunders needed a budget for a few dedicated vehicles and further, well-tailored development of the equipment and training. The sheriff's office didn't have the money, and experience had told him that he couldn't count on the police department to dedicate resources—especially not to another one of his lofty ideas.

Timeliness held the key. A new awareness of Alzheimer's disease, dementia and cognitive impairments, and attention to how to search for sufferers who wandered, had been emerging. Saunders and Rogerson met with representatives of local hospitals and organizations that served these populations. Perhaps they could help fund this promising solution to their critical common cause.

There the sense of purpose proved mutual and the idea was well-received, but the reverence didn't yield the revenue. The meetings did, however, raise affirmation and alliances. And comments that resonated with Rogerson inspired in him the name "Project Lifesaver." The positive energies coalesced, in Saunders' flexible ongoing appraisal of workability, as an alternative precious resource: the momentum needed to fuel ongoing pursuit.

In early 1999, Saunders approached members of Chesapeake General Hospital's charitable foundation for a grant of more than $150,000 to establish and launch the program.

"I really believe they thought I was crazy," he recalled. But he'd piqued their discretionary curiosity. The more details, confidence and urgency Saunders presented to them, the more follow-up information they requested. "I kept trying to tell them, 'Nobody's ever done this before, so anything I say is just going to be something I've invented,'" Saunders said, acknowledging how such a statement could alarm investors. "In retrospect," he admitted, "I can somewhat understand their reticence in saying, 'We're going to give this guy money to do *what?!*'"

A tireless run of multiple appeals finally resulted in the foundation granting Project Lifesaver $88,000 to seed a 15-month pilot. "I was elated," Saunders recalled. "OK, it wasn't what I'd asked for, but I got something." And he knew his strengths: From *something*, he could make *something more*. Just give him the grounds and plenty of room to grow.

The seed took root with Sheriff Newhart's help.

Saunders continued developing training specifically refined for his own unique model, which would still evolve organically as it progressed. Ingrained in his attitude as director of training for Chesapeake PD at the time was the idea that a Project Lifesaver training scenario should also satisfy law-enforcement certifications. "So I came up with one," he recalled, "and fortunately, they signed off on it. Probably because there was nothing else to compare it to," he joked.

With the foundational pieces in place, Saunders told Newhart they were ready to roll.

"The sheriff seemed pretty positive," Saunders recalled. "And I'll never forget what Dave Newby told him. He said, 'Now Sheriff, you need to understand something: You need to understand that once we start this, we can't stop it.'

"And the sheriff looked at me and said, 'Well, what do you think?'

"I said, 'Why would you *want* to?'

"He said, 'OK, go for it.'"

In April 1999, Chesapeake Sheriff's Office held a press conference to announce the launch of Project Lifesaver. Their demonstration, during which a simulated search resulted in the "lost" party being found within ten minutes, must have impressed the public. Saunders hadn't considered that the news would carry outside Chesapeake, but calls began pouring in from throughout southeastern Virginia, the very first request for service coming from a woman in Virginia Beach.

Her husband had dementia, and she couldn't rest. He stayed up all night, wandering around the house, and she feared that he'd wander off as she slept. The couple's door alarms might wake the wife, but only after her husband had gotten a head start out into the dark, the extreme heat or cold, or perhaps a nearby waterway.

While their plan had been to serve Chesapeake residents, Saunders and Newhart couldn't turn down their neighbors. Newhart said *do it*, and Saunders said *OK*.

Hence, placement of the first transmitter on that Virginia Beach gentleman April 9, 1999, marked the official founding date of

Project Lifesaver. Just as important, Saunders recalled of the wife's sentiments, "She finally felt like she could get some sleep."

Saunders and his team continued to answer the calls to place transmitter bracelets in surrounding cities.

NINE

Calling Out the Beast

"You know this is going to become a road show."

"What do you mean?"

*"This is gonna go all over the country, so
you'd better get your bags packed."*

Chesapeake and beyond, 1999-2005

Project Lifesaver agents had been fitting new clients throughout the region for three months before the first search-and-rescue call rang in July 1999, from their own city. A Chesapeake man with what Saunders refers to as medicinal dementia, brought on by treatments for terminal cancer, had gone missing again.

About two months earlier, prior to signing up with Project Lifesaver, the man had wandered from home. Saunders' team had found him nearly eight hours into a heavily involved search, along nearby railroad tracks less than half a mile from his house, exhausted and disoriented after having trekked amid high brush and some wooded terrain. The only reason they had been able to find him that quickly, Saunders recalled, was because a railroad engineer had spotted the man and radioed in the sighting.

Saunders had offered the new service to the man's wife following that rescue, and she had accepted. Now the gentleman had gotten away a second time, as a Project Lifesaver client.

"I remember getting the call," Saunders said. The event would prove or disprove everything for which he had prepared, everything he had set in place, everything he had promoted to benefactors, the sheriff, his agents, the press, the public and the desperate clients who had enrolled themselves or loved ones in this new expectant savior since April.

"OK," Saunders recalled thinking, "we've trained, we've practiced, of course we did what we thought we needed to do to be ready but now is where the rubber meets the road. So the anxiety was intense," he said. "You know, we're rolling in on this thing, and now this program makes it or breaks it, *right here*. Because if we don't find him, the program's worthless; it's a failure.

"And as I'm coming into the neighborhood," he continued, "I turned the receiver on, and I started getting the chirp through the receiver. Of course the anxiety level went down a lot then because I knew I had him.

"About a minute and half after I got out of the vehicle, I tracked him over to an apartment complex across the road. He had gone into the apartment hallway and into a storage closet under a stairway. So we tracked him into that closet. It took us about *a minute and a half* to recover him."

The fight had begun. Saunders had stirred the beast and pulled it into the ring. Round one had ended quickly and notably with a disruptive blow to his nemesis and a definitive victory for his brainchild.

"Once the story started getting out about that, you know, *the program works*, I felt much better," he recalled.

A public announcement spread news of the rescue. That generated more interest and increased client onboarding as calls poured in at a steady rate from cities surrounding Chesapeake.

Rogerson's wife, who owned a nail salon, couldn't help but talk up Project Lifesaver at work. One day, a local woman named Nancy Gray overheard her. Gray belonged to the Chesapeake club of Pilot International.

Founded in 1921 by forty-one Georgia businesswomen to influence positive change in local communities worldwide through fellowship, friendship and service, Pilot International encourages efforts toward brain-related health and safety, and actively supports people and organizations who care for others. Gray, who reportedly had served Pilot International in numerous elected positions, recognized the mission alignment between Project Lifesaver and

Pilot International and she spread the news to local chapters. Her club invited Saunders to speak, and he did. Impressed by the Project Lifesaver agenda, the group raised money to help support it.

TRAINING EXPANDS

Support for his brainchild was critical during its first twelve months, and Saunders gained timely tactical enhancement from a new initiative of Virginia Department of Criminal Justice Services. The DCJS had begun providing training to first responders across the Commonwealth in techniques for handling common calls that involved Alzheimer's and dementia patients. Saunders attended its first Alzheimer's trainer-to-trainer course, which deepened his knowledge and understanding of the clients he served while helping shape his own agent-training model. Duly, Chesapeake became the first police department in Virginia to institute Alzheimer's-specific training to its officers.

What's more, attending DCJS classes enabled Saunders to broaden exposure of Project Lifesaver to another naturally receptive audience.

"From then on, I had to go to every one of their training sessions and talk about Project Lifesaver," Saunders recalled. There, his sense of purpose, mission and execution prompted additional Virginia organizations to get involved.

Meanwhile, ongoing Project Lifesaver field training continued to reveal conditions that the old "tried-and-true" search methods couldn't effectively address.

"Gradually we started realizing that we needed to focus on more than just how to use the equipment," Saunders recalled. The more training and experience his team acquired, the more challenges they faced. *How to find an elusive signal? What if a client has a two- or three-hour head start and agents can't find a signal within thirty minutes of arrival?* "Then we moved into 'How do we deal with these people? How do we communicate with them?'" he said. "'How do we get a bracelet on those who resist?' You know, we started learning that you don't just walk in and slap a bracelet on somebody. What are some alternatives?"

A local nursing home held pearls of wisdom. To pluck them, Saunders would again have to jump out of the proverbial box. One or two at a time, dressed in civilian clothes and with permission, he and some of his agents began hanging around the memory lockdown area of the home's Alzheimer's wing. Without interfering or interacting with residents, they observed, listened, and gained what insights they could.

"That's when I learned about the 'greeter' at the doors," Saunders recalled. "The group that has dementia, they had become the self-appointed memory-care-unit 'greeters.' They'd be at the lockdown doors when a visitor comes in, and they say 'Hey, how're you doing? Have a good day,' you know, 'The nurses' station is over there,' or something. And then, before the door closes, *they're out!*" He laughed at the cunning.

"And that's where I learned, where it was really impressed upon me, that Alzheimer's patients are not dumb," he continued. "They have Alzheimer's, but they're not dumb. They haven't lost intelligence. They've lost some of the connectivity, at times, to be able to use that intelligence, or to recognize things, but often they're just as lucid and possess the same kind of skills that we have." The disease robs them, but not all at once, Saunders explained. "So you learn that you're dealing with intelligent people. The dementia is causing them problems in areas, yes, but they're not unintelligent."

Over the years he'd also realized that some patients, prior to wandering, talk about people, places, things or events that might clue others in to their motives and intentions. Paying attention to what they say at any given time gives caretakers conveyable information that might assist searchers in narrowing down predictable routes.

Saunders continued to merge his collective military, law-enforcement, search, and training expertise with newly acquired education about people with dementia to develop his own tactics, methodology and best practices. Whatever he learned, he shared.

As Project Lifesaver grew locally, Chesapeake Sheriff's Office continued responding to calls. But a single unit couldn't serve the exponential demand for very long. Saunders' team had been stretched thin by early 2000, when law-enforcement departments in other Virginia cities began requesting to replicate the program in service to their own communities. Saunders, who was more than happy to train them, developed a scalable three-day instructional model for the road.

"This is when the training module really started," Saunders recounted. "We'd trained our guys the way we thought they ought to be trained, but now we were going out there to train other agencies. This needed to really be a professional effort."

And it had been shaping up as such. Project Lifesaver's premier Electronic Search Specialist (ESS) course educated agents about the population with whom they would be engaging, and trained and certified them in this new special-focus ground search, equipment operations and running a Project Lifesaver division in their own departments. While the program had plenty of growth in its future, it was still the only one of its kind. And it had begun leading the field with authority.

In spring 2000, Saunders and his second-in-command, Rogerson, delivered the inaugural extra-departmental training to the Pittsylvania County, Virginia, Sheriff's Office.

"And I'll never forget what happened out there," Saunders said. "We're out in the field, training, and this young deputy says, 'You know this is going to become a road show.' I said, 'What do you mean?' He said, 'This is gonna go all over the country, so you'd better get your bags packed.' And he was so right."

The next request for training came from adjacent Virginia Beach, and Chesapeake Sheriff's Office took it on. Meanwhile, Newhart sought to appeal to the National Sheriffs' Association for Project Lifesaver endorsement. Such an alignment made obvious sense. "So we went to Washington, DC, and we presented it before their executive committee," Saunders recalled. "And everybody said, 'Yeah, yeah, I like that; we oughta do that,' except for one sheriff. It wasn't that he didn't like the program," Saunders said; "he said, 'No, we can't endorse this until it goes through the proper procedures,' which means it goes to the endorsement committee, then to the executive committee. We had skipped the endorsement committee, which he chaired.

"Ironically," Saunders continued, "within about two weeks after that, I get a call from him. He says, 'You know that program you talked about? How quick can you get it in my county?' That was Tuscaloosa County, Alabama."

But as Saunders planned that trip, he received a follow-up call from the same sheriff. "He said, 'You need to get down here,'" Saunders recalled. "'We just lost one in a lake.'"

Training for Tuscaloosa County commenced that summer. Then Saunders presented the program before the National Sheriffs' Association's endorsement committee, and they approved.

A HOME OF THEIR OWN

Chesapeake, Virginia, 2000/2001

As the year progressed, requests streamed in from sheriffs' offices in Kansas, Florida, West Virginia, Ohio and elsewhere in the country. Project Lifesaver needed a larger home—a separate facility for training and additional offices. Saunders put the word out and through a Navy SEAL contact discovered that the Navy's amphibious base in Norfolk had trailers they no longer needed. He was invited to take his pick and chose a large double-wide with several offices and a classroom. All he needed was a place to put it and a way to get it there. Around the start of 2001, Chesapeake Regional Airport provided a short-term location, and a local trailer company, whom Saunders called "a godsend," volunteered the relocation services. Agents from across the country began traveling to the new Project Lifesaver training facility, where Saunders' "baby" had the grounds to grow.

LEARNING TO FLY

Training and certifying out-of-state agents as Project Lifesaver Electronic Search Specialists and affiliates went well. But why stop at ground-search training, when you had also access to all that newly acquired air and landing space?

Still volunteering as a flight officer, Saunders had been broadening his birds-eye view of his mission, developing search-tracking procedures from helicopter. Now he had a site for perfecting protocol for an advanced course in airborne tracking for agents already certified as ESS.

The new Airborne Search Specialist course took search-and-rescue training to literal new heights.

Instruction ran the gamut, including: understanding helicopter characteristics; how to function safely within proximity of, and as approaching and entering, the vehicles; proper agent-pilot communication; safe and appropriate passenger conduct; and airborne search-tracking procedures, methodology and equipment operations.

Saunders executed extreme thoroughness, not only for the sake of his trainees and their clients, but also with respect for the pilots who would assist them. Pilots would require and deserve the assurance of, and the confidence in, the level of training and competence of the Project Lifesaver agents who would be conducting serious business in flight while the pilots conducted their own. On-the-job training would never be an option, nor would it be safe for anyone.

"Virginia Beach worked very well with me on training other agencies," Saunders recalled, citing the invaluable contributions made by Virginia Beach PD in providing the helicopter, pilots and essential professional insights for hands-on field training and simulations. Observer commentary delivered welcome validation: "We had a guy from the FAA actually sit in and audit the class and compliment us on our training, which I thought was pretty neat," Saunders recalled. Overall, "it worked out very, very well."

Once integrated, airborne tracking boosted search-ability to a range of five to seven miles.

The first airborne search commenced around spring 2002 after Saunders received a call from a woman that her father had taken off in his truck and was missing again. Saunders called for a helicopter. Assuming the role of flight officer, and along with two members of the 43rd, including Scott Nester, he boarded the vehicle. Saunders directed the pilot toward the North Carolina border where Nester got the RF signal. Sure enough, there was the truck. They radioed the ground team, who took it from there.

CRITICAL STRIDES

By 2001, Saunders' once-part-time voluntary mission had become a second full-time job—without pay. He and his fellow volunteers had been balancing everything at Project Lifesaver—from instruction to placing bracelets, changing their batteries and conducting the rescues—and the client-to-agent ratio had reached a tipping point.

He trained new agents in nearby Newport News, and by the end of day one, he recalled, he had received more than thirty voicemail messages from other agencies seeking the program. Saunders had already been spending his off-duty time from CPD on the road. The relentless demand inspired a new concept: a state-coordinator model, whereby Saunders and his sparse team of instructors would train one agreeable agency in each state, and those agencies would train others within their states in exchange for a portion of those program fees paid to Project Lifesaver. He developed three or four state coordinators accordingly while agency requests flew in from the West, Midwest and South.

While the increasing interest couldn't have pleased Saunders more, in time Project Lifesaver's inevitable growth and requisite travel had become unsustainable due to limited manpower and time. Fundraising had also become more cumbersome.

After nearly two years juggling the myriad logistical, physical and mental requirements of both jobs, Saunders struggled to fulfill increasing demand at Project Lifesaver. He could no longer operate effectively through the sheriff's office, a governmental agency. Two things had to happen.

First, Saunders had to choose between his history and longstanding career with the police force and his relentless vision of a purposeful future for Project Lifesaver.

"I talked to Jean and told her what I wanted to do, and for the first time, I got no argument from her about doing something," he joked in 2017. "She blessed it, and the next day I put in my papers for retirement."

On February 1, 2001, after thirty-three years on the force, Captain Gene Saunders walked away from Chesapeake Police Department to run full-time with Project Lifesaver, where he's always been known simply and affectionately as "Chief."

Second, to simplify things, train other agencies properly and operate most efficiently, Saunders had to reassess the efficacy of running his volunteer entity through a government agency. An attorney advised him to restructure it as a separate corporation. Saunders established the 43rd Virginia Search and Rescue Corporation but soon concluded that its for-profit status didn't align with the nature of his long-distance vision and burgeoning mission. Saunders wasn't in it to profit. And he'd realized that Project Lifesaver could expand more readily and help more needy agencies as a nonprofit, with the resultant access to grants and other funding opportunities that could help sustain operations and keep costs of equipment and program implementation down.

"So we let the for-profit go," he recalled. "And I said, 'OK, how do I apply for a 501(c)(3)?'"

Get an accountant. Get an attorney. And they write everything up and submit it, someone advised. "And I said, 'Oh, my God! How long does that take?'" Saunders recalled. "And they said, 'Well, it could take a year or two.'

"'Are you kidding me?!'" he countered. "I said, 'How much is a lawyer going to charge me for that?'

"'Well, you know, a couple thousand.'

"'I said, 'Oh, bull crap.'

"And you have to remember," Saunders continued, "here I am: a cop. I had never been a business man, I'd always been a cop. So I'm learning as I go. You know, the Columbus method: Seek and find. I have retired by now, and I'm taking this all on full-time.

"So I went online, and I printed up all the forms, and I sat down and I wrote it up myself. I figured, *What are they going to do, turn me down?* At least if they turn me down, maybe they'll tell me what I did wrong and I can redo it," he said. "So I wrote it up as I thought it should be, and I sent it in. And about three or four months later, I got a letter stating that we had been classified as a 501(c)(3) organization."

Determined, resourceful and unconventional, Saunders had wasted no time or money executing another critical task en route to his end goal. People probe, 'You what?! You didn't have a lawyer? You didn't have an accountant?' 'No,'" Saunders tells them. "What does that say?" he posed. "What that says is that *anybody* can do it." (Any-*bullheaded*-body with a heart full of tenacity, one could argue.) "Just sit down and do it."

2002-'03

As general demand and outreach continued to expand, Saunders recruited several state coordinators to travel to, and train, agencies outside their initially designated territories. In early 2002, in Saunders' own state of Virginia, newly elected Lynchburg Sheriff Ron Gillispie introduced Project Lifesaver to his staff to gauge their interest. Several of the deputies, including now-retired Captain Tommy Carter, had cared for parents with Alzheimer's disease, and others had children with autism. "So we all volunteered," Carter recalled in 2017. "We figured this would be a good thing."

Following successful staff recruitment by Gillispie, Saunders and Rogerson trained the new agents in Lynchburg. The team found the classes so interesting and exciting, Carter noted, that they extended the first day in the field for hours into the night.

Gillispie's volunteers all shared a purpose in becoming active participants, "and all of us were impacted as we saw that same passion in Gene Saunders when he taught the class," Carter recalled. The sentiment was unanimous: *This mission is personal.* And Saunders had been executing it as a consummate professional, Carter attested, citing the notable leadership acumen that Saunders had demonstrated in his teaching, presentation of the equipment and personal-professional interaction with the students.

Lynchburg Sheriff's Office kicked off its Project Lifesaver program to the community that year, and clients began enrolling immediately. "It wasn't long after that that we had one wanderer," Carter said. "That was Ola," he recalled, fondly. "She was ninety-two years old, and she was my sweetheart," one of his own clients. And she had referred to him as 'you good-looking devil,' he added, smiling.

According to Carter, it had hardly taken any time to locate his girl and return her safely. He had recognized the value in the program from the start, but once its impact had hit home, had struck his heart like the press of the kiss of immeasurable grace, he'd internalized it, he'd further personalized it, just as Saunders had done years earlier. And when Saunders asked him around the start of 2003 to assist him in training new agencies, Carter, backed by Gillispie's accommodative support, accepted. The timing couldn't have been better, as Rogerson retired that same year.

While assisting Saunders, Carter observed with awe the fluency, thoroughness and effectiveness with which Saunders trained emerging agents, and always without notes. Although the order in which he delivered them might vary, Saunders never missed a point. He had the ability to go with the flow of the group's energy while never veering off the track of his intended purpose, mission and ultimate goal.

This proved to be one advantage of the track being his own, another excursion from the dusty beaten path: Saunders, the avid champion for teamwork, had intuitively built his track with enough breadth and flexibility to accommodate and integrate the power of collective passion, enthusiasm and engagement. He knew that fuel to be a precious resource. The facts and details could be woven into a training in any number of ways, and he would ensure that they were. But to be most relevant, most indelible, most effective toward implementation, those facts and details had to also honor and yield to the transcendent elements of interpersonal relations, inspiration and demonstrative mutual respect and valuation. Those are integral components of success, often cultivated within the context of random, unplanned pockets of time and space that a visionary leader will understand, value and happily anticipate and for which he or she will add flexibility to the agenda.

Those truths aside, Saunders was one man. Carter knew that to properly develop protégés, they would need a well-organized compilation of the essential points condensed from Saunders' vast knowledge. Taking the initiative, he videotaped Saunders' classes on multiple occasions and translated the material to create a written training curriculum for ease of distribution and cohesiveness of instruction.

NEW GROUND

In 2004, Chesapeake Regional Airport had to reclaim its space to erect hangars. Project Lifesaver moved to a small site on Battlefield Boulevard where they found an ally in a generous and like-spirited landlord. Shortly after the move, two new contacts thrust the already racing organization into overdrive:

One night at home, Jean had asked if her husband had heard that Pauline Phillips, better known as Abigail Van Buren, author-creator of the "Dear Abby" syndicated advice column, had been enduring Alzheimer's disease. Phillips' family had announced it publicly in 2002.

Saunders hadn't heard. Jean suggested that he write her about Project Lifesaver. And he did.

Soon thereafter, Saunders received a call notifying him that the column, which had by then been being run by Phillips' daughter, Jeanne Phillips, would be publishing his letter. Within a week of it running, Project Lifesaver received several hundred new requests for information.

Another call, this time from television's *Extreme Makeover: Home Edition* followed.

"They were in Oak Park, Michigan, just outside of Detroit," Saunders recalled. "And they were doing an episode, rebuilding a house. Both parents were deaf, and one of the children had extreme autism and was a runner." In line with the show's philanthropic angle, "they asked if we could do anything with that."

Saunders said that he'd have to involve Oak Park Police Department, which, via numerous phone conversations, he arranged.

"So we went out there, and in combination of doing the show and putting the device on the child—and he was so sensitive, we actually devised pouches in the back of his clothes where they could put the tracking unit—we trained the police department," Saunders said. "We did all that in six days.

"And during the show, one of the cast members goes off somewhere, and Ty Pennington had surreptitiously put one of our tracking units in his back pocket. And now they're looking for him, and they can't find him, and they need him, and so they come and get me and say, 'Can you track him? He's got one of your units in his pocket.' So we track him about four blocks into a restaurant. And they showed that on the episode.

"It was a lot of fun," Saunders said. "And then, of course, the phones go wild."

The 43rd continued to run every aspect of Project Lifesaver from Chesapeake, even as the effort grew nationwide.

Saunders traveled so much that even Jean Saunders could hardly keep track. When asked where her husband was on any given day, she gave inquirers his cell phone number and suggested they call him and ask.

BREAKING BORDERS

2005 ushered breakthrough growth with the training of Project Lifesaver's first international agencies, located in Ontario, Canada. These were the Town of Caledon police, who requested the program, and the Ontario Provincial Police, who would be conducting most of the searches.

This milestone, while seemingly inevitable in light of its recent trajectory, had still been reached step by step of initiative, leap by leap of faith and push by push of tenacity. Deservedly, Project Lifesaver became *Project Lifesaver International.*

Carter, who had progressed in service from training assistant to national and airborne instructor, expanded his role to international instructor.

Television's *Discovery Channel* had gotten wind of the pending Ontario training and asked to film it for an episode featuring the program. Naturally, Saunders seized this rare opportunity for such valuable promotional media coverage. The more excitement and awareness generated around his mission, the better. He merged the production crew right onto his roomy track, and in this kiss of serendipity, everyone got what they needed that week.

Rick Derus, deputy chief of Ontario's Windsor Police Service, met Saunders while participating in that training. "My first impression of him was that he was a no-nonsense professional, totally committed to Project Lifesaver," Derus recalled in 2017. "I still remember him standing up in front of the classroom, and one of the things that struck me most was the strong presence he had that commanded the room. He was all business," despite the challenges inherent in expanding the burgeoning organization to international status, "and that has never changed with Gene," he said.

Derus would know. He has since worked closely with PLI, and in 2008 became its chairman of the Board of Trustees.

"I am always amazed to see how no obstacle is too difficult for Gene to tackle," he affirmed, referring primarily to the challenges that had unfolded following that year they met.

The same year, Saunders offered Carter a position as chief of training. But for that Carter would have to commute between Lynchburg and Chesapeake, some 200 miles each way.

Having lived in Lynchburg his whole life, having a home and a wife there, and having worked at the sheriff's office for thirty-two years, Carter had a lot to consider.

"This was the hardest decision I ever had to make," he said in 2017 from his office at PLI. "I asked him, 'I'm not going to get bored, am I? I don't like sitting still; I can't do that.'

"And Gene said, 'When you get here, just make sure you're running when your feet hit the floor.'" Carter shook his head and laughed. "And I said, 'OK, I can handle that; this'll work.'

"Based on the interactions I'd had with Gene, as well as the dedication I saw in him, I decided to retire and come to work for Project Lifesaver."

Carter retired from the sheriff's office and began weekly commutes as Project Lifesaver's chief of training. In time he'd be promoted to chief of operations and then chief of staff.

"And I can say now that there has never, ever been a day that I've come to work and said 'I'm all caught up, I think I'll take off, take a break,'" he said. "I've always had something to do. It's extreme."

THE HEART THAT BEATS THE DRUM

In the first six years since its inception, Project Lifesaver (International) trained and gained an average of more than 100 new agencies a year.

"We were just going like wildfire, as hard as we could go," Saunders recalled. If he'd had a larger crew, he could have advertised more, and "I'm sure we could have had more agencies and been even busier," he said. "But one of the things that I did not want to do was to get so big, so fast, that we lost sight of what we were doing and how we were doing it."

As always, Saunders continued to share what he learned via instruction, speaking and grass-roots promotion of Project Lifesaver. Over the years, collaboration and support came from myriad organizations, including: the International Association of Chiefs of Police, the National Sheriffs' Association, Autism Society, Autism Speaks, Alzheimer's Foundation of America, Aging in America, Rotary International, Lions Club, Grand (Masonic) Lodge of Virginia, Chesapeake city managers and numerous others and their positively immeasurable contributions.

As Nancy Gray continued to champion Project Lifesaver throughout Pilot International, the organization invited Saunders to speak at district, national and international meetings and conventions. The enthusiasm and assistance increased organically, evolving into what would become a lasting partnership between PI and PLI, and support from individual Pilot International clubs would remain steadfast, as critical in any given year as it had been in PLI's infancy.

Beneath Saunders' husk of tenacity must dwell a genteel and empathic sage. Many have noted his propensity for offering, attracting and sustaining relationships of sweeping mutual benefit, whose whole he foresees will be greater than the sum of its parts. This vitalizes a major cog in the machine of perpetuity at Project Lifesaver International. And through the heart of the cog flows a quickening stream of good intentions fortified by all who subscribe to the vision, the cause and the mission.

For those who have teamed up to wrangle the rapacious nature of the beast they all know, Saunders' respect, admiration and gratitude run as deep as the cache of memories suppressed and as pervasive as the stream of righteous intention that pumps from the heart of the cog.

TEN

A Bull in Hell

"You're going to know when you're over the target . . ."
"What do you mean?"
"Everybody's going to be shooting at you."

—*Chief Gene Saunders' recollection of cautionary*
comment by Sheriff Jim O'Sullivan

No great feat goes unchallenged. That's predetermined; that's *inherent*. For it's the catalytic challenges, and how they're faced, that shape what will ultimately define the greatness of the feat.

Beginning with Project Lifesaver's inception, Saunders had expected to wrestle the garden-variety beasts: team and resource management, fundraising, organizational logistics and standard operational gridlock.

What he hadn't anticipated was that beasts of the human kind—the cannibals he'd thought he'd left behind in retirement from the underbelly—so insidiously trolled the seemingly tame and gentle world of nonprofit humanitarianism, as well. That was a hell of a wake-up call, the mere recollection of which still burned his ass in 2017.

2006-'09

As positive energy continued to fuel Project Lifesaver International's expansion, Saunders stayed attuned to organizational undertones.

Among the most essential of these were the people and the equipment in which he'd placed his trust.

Proper development of any kind requires reliance on those one trusts. That said, the trust must derive from trust*worthiness*.

"When we first started, we were the only game in town," Saunders recalled. But had he ever taken predator-speak as a second language, he'd have known that the designation can also translate to *the freshest blood in the pool*. "What we learned is there was always somebody who came along and wanted to push us out of business. They wanted to do away with us or our support system because we were their competition," he explained. "As this thing started growing, and they saw what they thought was a large market—which wasn't really the case—they wanted to take it over. And they either did it by betrayal or by attempted sabotage. I learned in those instances what competitors will resort to, to get what they want."

The trend began with one of his manufacturers evidently developing a taste for blood in the wake of its own unaccountability for Saunders' emerging needs.

"I wanted to constantly improve things," Saunders recalled. "Not necessarily *change* things," he clarified, because change without good cause made no sense to him, "but if your equipment's at one level, let's always work to make it better. And let's listen to the guys and girls in the field who are using it to tell us how we can make it better and easier and more efficient."

By 2006, feedback from the field had begun to raise concerns. Agents reported equipment failures caused by moisture, primarily receivers short-circuiting in rainy or misty weather and transmitters failing due to leakage when exposed to water as clients immersed them while swimming or wandering. Saunders and Carter approached the manufacturer about waterproofing, but to no avail.

"We kept asking them, prodding them, to improve it, and they kept coming back with suggestions like 'wrap it in a balloon' or 'cover it with a plastic bag,'" Saunders said.

Hence, he and Carter entertained the perennial workaround, attempting a range of quasi solutions from collecting hotel-room shower caps to later protect receivers from the rain to finding a secondary manufacturer of watertight transmitter cases to replace those being supplied by their primary manufacturer.

The entertainment value quickly waned.

In time, field complaints included heavy signal interference while operating on the designated 215 MHz frequency in some locations. Saunders first experienced the issue in Lynchburg.

"We were trying to track a transmitter, and there was so much background and static and white noise, it was extremely difficult to hear the transmitter chirp," he recalled. "We couldn't figure out what the issue was, and when we went back to the company, they came up with a lot of stopgaps on how to fix it." But from band-pass filters to the general runaround, no "fix" proved reliable.

By 2008, the ongoing effort seemed extraneous. Saunders was in the life-saving business. For that, he counted on professionals in the manufacturing business to acknowledge his needs and offer solutions. "So we started looking around," he recalled.

He met with a Canadian manufacturer at a conference in Massachusetts and found that company's equipment to be superior. Smaller, waterproof, easier to handle and more sensitive to signals, it addressed his challenges. Furthermore, this was all-digital, unlike the current line's technology which was analogue, he said.

With analogue equipment, signals from transmitters tended to float, drifting sometimes two to five kilohertz up or down, depending on the atmosphere and the environment, from the designated frequency, he explained.

"For instance," he said, "if I'm trying to tune in to 215.210, I may have to go to 215.213 to actually get it. Tomorrow I might get it at .211. The next day I may get it at .209. So we might have to run a span of eight to ten frequencies in order to find it. But digital usually locked right in to the frequency we were looking for." All things considered, he said of the newly presented equipment, "we liked it."

According to Saunders, PLI's contract with its existing manufacturer stated that he could supplement his current line of equipment with that made by other manufacturers if he gave the existing manufacturer a specified amount of time to meet the new standard and deliver the same. If the original company delivered, PLI would stay with it.

"So we notified them that we got this equipment," Saunders said. "We were going to continue using them and using the new equipment, allowing these older guys, under the contract, to come up to speed to the new equipment.

"Well, they didn't take it well," he continued. "They sued us—breach of contract and I don't know how many other things." Despite the fact that their equipment had been underserving a population whose lives depended upon it, "they would rather sue us, and force us to use their stuff, than abide by the agreement," Saunders moaned. "So we decided 'That's it,' we're going all to the new manufacturer's equipment if they were going to be that way."

Turning his attention to the Canadian manufacturer, Saunders caught a break. During conversations about past interference in the 215 MHz band, someone asked if he was aware that the band had been sold to HDTV.

That explained everything. "It was like the bell rung," Saunders said. "Every time we got around a transmission tower belonging to certain stations, it would wipe out our 215 band. Because they were transmitting high-definition TV signals in the 214/215 band."

Saunders approached the Federal Communications Commission, who directed him to switch to 216 MHz, a band that was phasing out wildlife tracking, having been newly designated for use by law-enforcement for tracking systems related to criminal activity. Good solution overall, but that meant that in some parts of the country 216 still served wildlife tracking. And the manufacturer suing PLI took full advantage of the fact.

"Aside from suing us, they were advertising to our members and prospects everything they could think of to smear our name," Saunders said. "They started advertising that you don't know if you're tracking Grandma or a coyote, Grandma or a bear. They were trying to undermine us."

Saunders and the new manufacturer had already resolved that issue by encoding the transmitters to signal the receivers that they were tuning into, or tracking, the correct device. But the old manufacturer continued the smear campaign, accusing the new manufacturer of producing inferior equipment, Saunders said. Lawsuit, lies and all, "they called the sabotage 'competition.'"

Why any intelligent business person would see a hard-working, small-staffed nonprofit—whose entire gig revolved around profiting just enough to fuel a mission bent on giving all it can to its beneficiaries—as "competition" in the for-profit world made no sense to Saunders. But that mentality was 'not his circus, not his monkeys,' as the saying goes.

Saunders and his team continued defending Project Lifesaver. Meanwhile, if sabotage from an *external* source wouldn't break him, perhaps betrayal from the *inside* would.

That same year, upon his return from a conference in Phoenix, Arizona, Saunders received an email from a PLI board member asking if he'd gotten "in over his head." The email contained accusations brought by a senior staff member of dishonorable behavior by Saunders, as detailed in a list of things that he had allegedly "done wrong" in recent years. Saunders erupted.

"I was pissed," he recalled. "First off, I had been blindsided. Second, I didn't appreciate that my staff member, without saying a word to me, would go to the board with all these allegations that I knew nothing about."

Saunders called an emergency board meeting where he stepped down as board chairman, Derus stepped in, and Saunders told them all regarding the instigator: "*I'm* leaving or *this guy's* leaving. I'm not going to be in the same building with him because none of this stuff is true."

That same night, the staffer left his assigned vehicle in the PLI parking lot, with everything that had been issued to him locked inside, and left his keys and a letter of resignation at the front desk. When business resumed, Carter was promoted to chief of operations.

But despite their steadfast respect and admiration for Saunders, the board had no choice but to examine the allegations. They contained charges of corruption and criminal intent, including fiscal misconduct and behavior that could, theoretically, enable embezzlement.

"So, alright, here they go," Saunders recalled. "They're now investigating me, looking at everything I've done." For about the next twelve months, a team intent on uncovering the truth about the accusations would scrutinize every relevant detail of Saunders' daily operations of the recent past—from his credit card use and fund management to his mail-opening habits. "It put me and my wife through a year of hell," he said. His tone underscored the latent sentiment: *Unforgiveable.*

Meanwhile, the legal battle with the disgruntled manufacturer continued to fester despite tamping by countersuits from PLI.

Finally, in 2009, team Project Lifesaver delivered the blow that broke the plaintiffs' back: the threat of a class-action lawsuit by affected PLI member agencies, based upon the discovery that the manufacturer had been notified by the FCC more than a decade earlier about the source of interference on the 215 MHz band and, with complete disregard for PLI's legitimate concerns and repeated inquiries, had been withholding the vital information.

"Well, at that point, I think they realized that we were serious and we were going to pull the big guns out," Saunders recalled. "They decided they wanted to settle." After all the time, money and energy spent on something that never should have happened, "nobody got anything," he said. "We just walked away from each other and said *that's it; done. You go your way, and we'll go ours.*"

According to Saunders, that company continued to undermine Project Lifesaver. "But what they fail to understand," he noted, "is that anyone with any intelligence is going to question, 'How come they're not still using you?'"

That year, the tables of justice also turned on the internal investigation front. The facts hadn't been aligning with the implications.

"The board had started realizing, as I understand it, that things aren't what they're being told," Saunders said. "They started finding out that all these allegations were wrong, they had no factual base."

The team began questioning the motives of the instigator. And one of the board members ascertained the real lowdown. According to the findings, the staff member had been in cahoots with a wealthy acquaintance of Saunders who sought to take over Project Lifesaver.

"The guy instituted a coup using my high-ranking employee," Saunders said. "And they were going to do it by pushing me out through accusations of misconduct." The man with the money had planned to install the staffer as a figurehead CEO and dictate operations as the "silent leader," Saunders explained, "so they decided that every mistake I've ever made—and I've made mistakes—they're going to throw out there, and they're going to have the board get rid of me."

In the end, "everything was proven to be an out-and-out lie," Saunders said. And although he had triumphed in both battles in the paired ordeals, the residue would stick around for a while like slime from a slug. That trail began with a call from a reporter looking to do a story on Project Lifesaver. Saunders agreed to an interview, unaware of the negative nature of the inquiry.

"When we met, he said, 'I've gotten this information, and I'm going to do an investigative report on it,'" Saunders recalled. "I had nothing to hide, so I sat there with him for three and a half hours, talking to him, answering every question he wanted, telling him everything he wanted to know," he said. "But it was like talking to a wall," and Saunders couldn't help but wonder why, he said, especially in light of all the positive accounts and information he'd been sharing. Nearly ten years after the story ran, he still had his suspicions about who had pitched it—negative angle and all—to a reporter who Saunders believes should have been more astute. PLI didn't pursue legal action. "We were in no shape to start a whole new legal thing and spend money on lawyers again," he said. "So we just decided to take the high road—the people who knew us knew us, we had a lot of letters to that effect in support of us, and fortunately it all turned out OK."

But a decade later Saunders still referred to that time as "one of the worst years in my life."

EMBERS ON HIS TAIL

There ain't no rest for the weary along the road of good intentions. As the dust of the past year's *haboob* had been kicked up, whirring and finally settling down, his Canadian supplier had gone into receivership and been acquired by another company.

Still, Saunders had no reason to anticipate trouble. He had been assured that everything would remain the same, all the company wanted to do is make and supply the equipment, he recalled. "Then they called us to a meeting in Boston," he said. "And we weren't there five minutes before we knew this thing had gone off the rails." Saunders shook his head. "My wife was with me, and a couple of the other guys in the company, and right away it was very apparent that what they'd said and what they were doing were two different things." Now he was suspicious.

"The first thing Jean had noticed was that our logo on their brochures had become about the size of the end of my little finger. You couldn't even tell what it was. And they'd renamed the program," as if it had ever been theirs to rename. "So we could see then that this was not going to be a great partnership," Saunders said. "They wanted to 'restructure' our model and take it over.

"Well, we pushed back," he continued. "And it became a pushback all the time. They wanted to redo the entire program, they wanted to do it a different way, and I kept telling them it's not going to work that way."

The push and pull continued for almost a year before Saunders and Carter met with the manufacturer again, this time for a planning session to discuss how to proceed in the future.

"So we get in there, and we find out what their 'plan' was," Saunders recalled. "They handed us a letter terminating the contract, telling us that we could still buy equipment from them but they were going to take and handle all the large customers, all the major cities and the big metropolitan areas, and we can have what's left."

The manufacturer had been redeveloping Saunders' model as its own and had planned to sell directly to customers, he explained. He glared through an incredulous pause. "All the larger agencies that had the most clients, they were going to take them," he said. "And come to find out, for several weeks prior, they had been wining and dining a number of our large agencies, going around meeting with them, telling them this was coming."

If his unfortunate introduction to the world of bait-and-switch hadn't done much else for Saunders, it had honed his hackles. Because he'd already been suspicious, Project Lifesaver had been seeking other avenues of supply. Soon PLI began relying on other sources and replaced that supplier without further issue.

NOT SO FAST, CHIEF

As Saunders kept his eye on what emerging technologies he could add to his armory in his quest against the beast, one company looked promising: its equipment connected through a system of cellular triangulation. Following multiple demonstrations, he introduced it to the field.

In addition, the new company asked Saunders to train other customers in the use of its devices in exchange for monthly payments reflective of Project Lifesaver's operating budget, understanding the value of his support of their products within his existing line. That sounded to Saunders like a mutually beneficial arrangement, so he agreed.

But in time, as problems emerged with the new equipment and its manufacturer pushed for exclusivity in his product line, Saunders had to reconsider.

His agents had begun reporting issues, including signal and communications inconsistencies. Saunders told the manufacturer that he thought the technology might work well in some areas but was "not worth a damn" in others, and he wasn't going to support it anywhere he knew or believed it wouldn't operate effectively.

Then he discovered the need to "wake up" the equipment prior to demos. "It would 'sleep' for a while, and then it would wake up and kind of look out and say 'Is anybody trying to get ahold of me?'" he explained. "As it's sleeping, it's not going to talk to you," he said. That wasn't the continuous functionality that he'd been led to believe it was. "So I see what's happening, and I'm pushing back: 'This is not what we agreed to,'" he said. "Their message was that their technology was far more advanced and far more reliable, and it wasn't. And I refused to comply.

"I think they wanted their technology to replace what we were doing," Saunders continued, citing an eventual discovery: "We would be talking to an agency about Project Lifesaver, and if we mentioned it to our equipment manufacturer, we'd find out that they would go in behind us and take over. They would put their stuff in there and never tell us about it.

"Well, from then on, it was just one thing after another with these guys," Saunders said. During a trade-related conference, he had what he called a "pretty hefty argument" with one of the supplier's senior people. "We're standing in a restaurant, and he starts talking about equipment and saving lives," he recalled. "He accused me, 'Don't you want to save lives?' and I said, 'Yes. But I want the equipment to be able to do it.' Well, you could tell that during that whole conference, there was a big cold shoulder. Something was going on; I didn't like it," he said. "The cop hackles were up. And I told my staff that until we've ironed this out, they were not to have anything to do with them. And then I notice that one of my staff is not acting right. Contrary to my directions, on the last day of the conference, she's putting this guy in our car, taking him to the airport!

"I knew then that something was really wrong," Saunders said. "There was no doubt, because she was the liaison between us and them. Well, I hadn't realized it yet, but this girl had become their spy and was tight with their CEO. She was telling them about internal communications; she was reporting back to them." The following Monday morning, Saunders called her into his office. "She knew right then that she was going to be terminated," he said.

He fired her, and she demanded her paycheck. He told her she could have it when she returned everything that had been issued to her. But that didn't go over well.

"She returned with a garbage bag full of stuff and threw it into my office," Saunders said. "So I give her her paycheck, and she starts to holler and scream. I told her, 'Get out. You are now put on notice that you're trespassing. Leave now or I'm calling the police.' Well, she got all huffy and she stomped out. But before she left, she screamed, 'You're going down, and you're going down hard! Mark my words!' Then she slammed the door so hard it shook the building.

"Well, that was the big blow-up," Saunders said. "And the next thing I know, we're getting sued! That day, we get notice of a federal lawsuit against us—breach of contract, fraud, blah, blah, blah. So then I'm calling the attorneys. We're going into countersuit mode."

Saunders had Carter search the employee's office computer. "We found out that she had wiped it clean," he said. "So we go into the server and find all kinds of emails where she had been colluding with that company, giving them sensitive information, privileged information. We found out she was also stealing information from the office and taking it back to her home and sending it to them. And she had been corresponding on a more intimate level with the CEO."

The woman was arrested and eventually convicted of computer trespass. But the court battle between PLI and the supplier would wage for nearly a year.

"It got to the point that it was really looking bleak," Saunders said of the suit. "And it was getting expensive because we had to protect ourselves." But as motions stacked up against the supplier, team PLI gained ground. "Finally it occurred to me, 'I'm tired of this crap,'" Saunders said. "So I tell the lawyer, 'Here's what I want you to do: They claim that they've got such good stuff, I want you to make a motion that we want to see every time one of their units was turned on—anywhere in the world, for any reason, from the time it was invented until now, I want the results of that turn-on. How many times did they do it, and was it a failure, or was it a success?' I knew their stuff wasn't working," he said, "and I wanted a report, a printout, of every time they turned one of their units on and what the result was."

His attorney petitioned the court, and the court ruled against the manufacturer. "They fought back," Saunders said. "They did not want to supply that. And the judge said *oh, yes, you will!* They had to furnish it. Well, they wanted to come to the table then; all of a sudden they wanted to talk about negotiation. We ended up settling for an undisclosed amount, most of which went to the lawyers. And then they walked away and we walked away. To this day, part of the settlement was that we could never see those results."

Saunders has since learned that the manufacturer had been a second-tier subsidiary of one of the largest conglomerates nationwide. Like others, "their intent was to push us out of the market, put us out of business, and take us over," he said. "Because we were their 'competition.' Apparently they figured that if we weren't around, they would be the only game in town. *So let's minimize them. Let's gradually push them into nonexistence. They don't want to go willingly? We'll sue them into nonexistence.*"

The predatory practice still seemed surreal to Saunders, years later. "They had a history of going in, partnering with small companies, pissing them off, suing them, and forcing them out of business, financially, so that they could then take over," he explained. "Smaller organizations just get to the point that they can't afford to fight them anymore, and they give up. So if you're a small, little nonprofit corporation like us, and you've got one of the biggest conglomerates in the country pouring in money to get rid of you, well, that's a little daunting."

But again, he'd taken on a beast for the sake of the vulnerable. "At the end of this negotiation my lawyer said, 'Well, you didn't make any money, but look at it this way: You beat back one of the largest conglomerates in the country.'

"I said, 'How nice.'" Saunders laughed at the irony before his expression turned serious. "While that may be some consolation," he said, "look at the money we spent. And how long was it going to take us to recover?"

Dealing with multiple lawsuits took a serious toll, not only on Saunders but on the entire organization. "It was tough," he said. "It's not something that happens and then goes away overnight. It was tough keeping things going from one day to the next. And for every lawsuit, I had to come up with a strategy to outsmart them, to get around them. Apparently they had been trying to bleed us financially, and regardless of what you do when you are in litigation, it's expensive." According to Saunders, Project Lifesaver International spent more than $400,000 in legal fees on two lawsuits. "And that was more to defend ourselves than anything else," he said. "The lawyers were good to us," he affirmed, "but we still had to pay them. And because we're nonprofit, that was money that I really regret that we had to spend. To think what I could do with that money today—or then."

Saunders would like for nobody who needed the service to ever have to pay for it. Back then, what he had to spend on legal entanglements represented close to PLI's annual budget, and could have liberated agencies and clients of the bulk of their program costs.

"It's taken us a long time to recover from the last one," Saunders said. "You know, people don't understand that everything doesn't go back to square one when these things are over. You have to rebuild." PLI had depleted all of its financial reserves. That affected the organization's ability to purchase and maintain inventory and ship it in a timely manner. "Once the litigation was over, and we were able to sit back and lick our wounds, we had to redirect and look at our planning and how we were going to be able to get the inventory back up, which was a very slow process because if you don't have cash, you can't get inventory," he explained. Governmental agencies don't pay as quickly as other customers do because of the bureaucracy and oversight involved, he added, "and that means there's no cash flow coming in for us to purchase inventory, to restock our inventory, and to send out orders. Naturally, some of the agencies started to question how long it was taking to get equipment. We had to get that inventory back up so there wouldn't be a lag time in filling the requests from the members. So it slowed everything down, which caused us a lot of frustration, caused our members frustration, and we had to work really, really hard to overcome that. It was a very slow, painstaking process."

Carter, a self-proclaimed micromanager, concurred. While Saunders had been off in court, he had struggled to pay the bills and helped to keep the organization running as smoothly as possible. "Neither one of us was willing to back away from the pressure, that's all there was to it," he said. Despite the strength and endurance of the storm, Carter had refused to view his station as a sinking ship. Instead, he recognized areas of need and took responsibility for whatever he could do—an attitude he'd developed in his formative years from his parents' instilling that "If you're going to do something, do it right and do it well," and one of his most memorable bosses training him that "There's always something to do; if you see something that needs fixing, go ahead and do it."

His wife hadn't thought he'd last a year with the weekly commute, never mind adversity like this, "But I'm kind of like a bulldog," Carter said. "If I bite into something, if I make a commitment, I'm going to do it. And I wasn't about to let anybody beat down what Gene had worked hard to build."

"No," Carter reiterated, "they were not gonna beat us on this."

PLI was like any really good thing: its environment might have changed some, but the core of its culture had not. The experiences that had tested the people of PLI in those years only amplified their intentions, their fortitude, their resourcefulness and other integral attributes, making the small-but-mighty team that much stronger, more focused and more cohesive.

"We had to do a lot of soul-searching, belt-tightening, and reevaluating how and why we were doing some things," Saunders recalled. "There were three years that I gave employees raises and I didn't take one, because they were working hard. I mean, they were really doing everything they could, and then some.

"But there just wasn't enough money to go around," Saunders continued. "And I had to cut it from somewhere."

Cutbacks pertained mostly to travel, conference participation, and staff size yielding to natural attrition. "So all of that played into how we operated," Saunders said. He and Carter routinely reassessed the budget: What could they move around? What could they reprioritize? What could they *not* do until finances improved? "It was a constant tradeoff-kind of thing, and plenty of cutting and slashing, just so that we could make sure that our members got the equipment as quickly as we could get it to them," he said. "After all, our whole mission is to get that stuff out there, and get the training out there, to protect these people."

THE RUB

Those years were hell, Saunders said. The scorching commonality among the beasts had apparently not been the desire to partner for good or work together for a common cause. Oh, no, that altruism had been the mark of the bygone Boy Scout years; that "loyalty" expectation thing was merely a mental token of his "brother-SEAL" phase. Deceit marked the new-world beast, and that game had been on before he knew he'd signed up for it. He wouldn't *really* be their *teammate*; they had to make him their *competition*. That's how they rolled: push the little guys off the playing field, out of the game, out of their way.

Those were the days that beat his rookie ass, "the mornings when you got up and you really had to push yourself to get out of bed and come to work," Saunders said. "And you dread it because you feel like, *what's gonna happen today?*" He leaned forward across the edge of his desk. "But my position was, we weren't giving up," he declared. "No, we hadn't done anything wrong, and we weren't going to capitulate. We weren't going to be swallowed up by a giant. I felt like we had something good, it was working, it was doing the job. And now we've got these guys wanting to drive us out and take over." He shook his head. "I wasn't going to have it," he said. "Every one of them, we were in the right. We fought tooth and nail against what we have been told were just horrendous odds, in each one of them."

It's not easy to overcome those odds and all the compounded pressure, Saunders said. You question yourself. You second-guess your physical, mental and emotional stamina, your fortitude. You wonder if what you're doing *really* matters to others as much as you've always believed it has, and as much as it matters to you. "But you just have to pull yourself out of the bleakness and say, 'We are trying to accomplish something, and we are going to keep moving ahead,'" he said. "Regardless. We're going to keep forging ahead. And we're just gonna fight it. We're gonna fight it with everything we've got."

It's a *decision*. And with all the feelings that can get in the way, when decision-making time comes a person must give as much analysis to the positive feelings that set the thing in motion as he does to the feelings conjured by the forces trying to stop it. And if those positive feelings still ring legitimate and worthy, and if they still represent a gut-level understanding of transcendental potential, those are the feelings from which to draw the power to rise above the circumstances *du jour* in order to realize the vision of tomorrow.

Yes, the betrayals hurt, Saunders said. But the man knows how to reframe a perspective. He recalled an ominous comment by Chesapeake Sheriff Jim O'Sullivan, then CSO chief deputy:

"Jim O'Sullivan told me one time, 'You know, you're going to know when you're over the target,' meaning when you've got it, and you're successful, and you're doing what you need to be doing.

"I said, 'What do you mean?'

"He said, 'Because everybody's going to be shooting at you.' In other words, you become the target.

"And that's exactly what happened," Saunders said. "Every time we thought that we were moving ahead, we found people who wanted to get us out of the way. They felt like there was big money in what we were doing, and as much as I told them there was no big money, it didn't matter. They had these delusions of grandeur; they were going to make 'big money.' I said, 'I don't think so,' but they didn't believe me. I said, 'You can get by, yes, you can get by; you can make enough money to pay your bills and pay your salaries, as long as you don't over-extend, but what you're talking about is just not out there. It's just not there.'"

A smile slipped its way into Saunders' conclusive reflection. "Since then," he said, "we've been doing OK." He laughed with pride and relief. "That was part of our growing pains. And even at that, we're still here. So what does that say?

"When I try to step back and see it objectively," he continued, "I think that one of the primary messages we could try to put across is that up until now, no matter what anybody's thrown at us, we've overcome. We fought back and kept going, with the confidence that we were doing something good, and they weren't going to put us down for whatever their motives were.

"It's been a learning experience—sometimes a very unpleasant learning experience," Saunders concluded. "I like to have good harmony in everything that I do, and it really bothers me when things happen like have happened in the past. It took a long time to recover. We are still feeling it sometimes. And it brought up a resolve in me that I am not going to be screwed over. *Just not.* But hopefully, as they say, because of this we've grown stronger, we've grown smarter."

PARACHUTE PACKERS

"My wife says she's surprised I escaped with my sanity," Saunders said. But he knows he wouldn't have survived at all without Jean and others who believed in him and embraced the mission.

"Thank God I had a board who supported me," he said. "And my wife, who was my rock and confidante, assured me every day that we would overcome this, we just had to keep pushing forward and not allow anything to overcome us.

"And Tommy," Saunders continued, "who was tremendous in locating information pertinent to the situation and was crucial in helping keep the organization functioning and on an even keel.

"And other people who hung in there with me—if it hadn't been for all of them, I don't know . . ."

With all the chaos, "the attitude of the staff was great," Saunders continued. "We were not the highest paying jobs around, for a lot of different reasons: the cash-flow problems, and those kinds of things. But while some left for higher-paying jobs elsewhere, I know staff who had the opportunity to leave and didn't," he said. "I think they were in it because they felt like it was something good to be doing, it was helping people, and they weren't in it so much for the money. Because let's face it: When an organization goes through some of the things we were going through, regardless of the face you put forth, the stress still shows. It's still there. You know, you can be the jolly old man, upbeat and all that, but people know. They're not dumb. They know there are underlying problems. When you're in the midst of a gigantic lawsuit, they know. They know the stress. They know the lawyers are calling, they know all the stuff. They may not know all the minute details, but they know the organization is stressed.

"But they kept on doing their job," Saunders said of his employees. "They just handled it as it came, and it didn't matter whether it fit their job description or not; they just did it. And they did it very well. They even pitched in and did extra.

"And we had to *work*!" he attested, laughing. "When people say *work harder with less*, listen, we could give you lessons in that! And we still do a lot of that," he said of PLI's current culture. "I mean, nobody here wears one hat. We all wear four or five hats. I just got through vacuuming and dusting and cleaning the office," he said. "So we just do what has to be done to get it done. I'm at bare-bones staff, and it's pretty much going to stay that way for the foreseeable future."

Ultimately, Saunders said upon reflection, "I think we got through it because we were hard-headed and God was on our side." And every agency, organization and individual on Earth who has supported him and the organization has been a godsend. When put on the spot to name only a few in 2017, Saunders hated not to tout the immeasurable impact of, and his infinite gratitude for, every single one of them. For time's sake, he mentioned one organization and one individual who reflected his affinity for all.

"One of the biggest cheerleaders we ever had was Pilot International," Saunders said. "I always knew that if I really wanted something done, just let the Pilots get hold of it. And even when we had the big problems, I spoke before their executive council on three or four occasions and they stuck with us. They stood by us. They are tremendous people, tremendous ladies," he attested, "and they still work with us today.

"A lot of other people have just really grabbed hold and really gotten out there as well," Saunders continued. It's humbling, reaffirming and motivating all at once, he said. "And when you see people who come forward like Martha Lieberman, well, she's an inspiration by herself . . .," and a *whole 'nother story . . .*.

ELEVEN

Making the Case

"It's all about tenacity. Don't give up."

—Martha Lieberman

According to Martha Lieberman, her mother had never hit anyone over the head with her cane—"although she threatened to."

Lieberman yielded briefly to the laughter of her audience at the 14th Annual Project Lifesaver International Conference, held in Orlando, Florida, in August 2017. More than 100 member agents, volunteers, advocates and organizers from throughout North America had convened for the latest educational insights, technology updates, training, networking and more.

Lieberman—head of the Lehigh Valley, Pennsylvania, Project Lifesaver program—offered her special brand of encouragement, inspiration and ironic wit, drawing partly from the indelible influence of her mother, Judith Lieberman, and partly from her own experiences banging her head against the walls of indifference and inertia for more than a decade.

Judith Lieberman had initiated the effort to establish Project Lifesaver in Pennsylvania in 2004, beginning with her home region of Lehigh County. Since Judith's death at age ninety-three in Sept. 2013, her daughter has spearheaded continuation of the relentless efforts of the late tenacious matriarch. At the conference, she shared the good, the bad and the utterly maddening, along with some keys to her eventual successes in the ongoing push.

"The struggle to bring Project Lifesaver to Pennsylvania has been a very long, painful process," Lieberman said. "It's a very involved story.

"The program started in about 2004, and we ran into a lot of problems back then," she continued. By 2009 "we had two departments that were trained, bracelets were handed out, financing, state grants in place, and one day the sheriffs from two departments decided, for no reason that we know, to pull the rug out from under us."

According to a WFMZ-TV news report, Lehigh County proclaimed to have dropped the program over "logistical red tape."

"All of a sudden, we were taking bracelets back," Lieberman recalled. "Finances again were in question, and nobody wanted to know Project Lifesaver. They didn't want to hear about it because it was all negative."

Still unsure what had transpired to create the abrupt shift, Lieberman clearly remembered her mother's response to the offense: goaded and blessed *chutzpah*. Rather than become disheartened— or heaven forbid, *defeated*!—Judith Lieberman became a more fixed, brazen, outspoken, cane-wielding presence for the cause. As Lieberman assisted her, the awe for her mother grew pervasive and impassable. And if tenacity is contagious, she was catching more than her share from prolonged exposure.

"There isn't a step-by-step" for getting PLI to catch on among the un-indoctrinated, Lieberman told attendees. But opportunities abound for those who recognize them and think and act with creativity, common sense and innovation.

She cited the break that changed everything in terms of her ability to further communicate through the media regarding Project Lifesaver: In February 2011, a gas explosion killed five of her neighbors. Bo Koltnow, a reporter with WFMZ-TV news serving eastern Pennsylvania and western New Jersey, interviewed her. As irrelevant as it seemed at the time, the event introduced Lieberman to the reality that she could reach out to him again. The following year, she knew who to call when standing up to the mayor regarding a safety improvement to a traffic light at a dangerous intersection for which she had been fighting city hall. That fight had strengthened her civic spunk, and her outspokenness earned her the media coverage.

"The news reporter finished his interview after I'd called the mayor a liar," she recalled, "and his final comment was, 'Beware, city hall. Martha Lieberman has a lot of tenacity and will be back.' He had no idea how true that was."

Lieberman had earned new respect, and the news-related interactions helped to establish a positive rapport between her and Koltnow as she further refined her sense of media savvy. "And as a result of that," she said, "he's become my personal newsman for Project Lifesaver. All I have to do is pick up the phone and say, 'Hey, Bo, we've got this going on,' and Bo is there doing it."

Lieberman recalled her first PLI-related pitch to Koltnow around late 2012: "A mother had contacted me," she said. "Her daughter had been found a couple of times climbing the fence onto the busiest highway that goes through Lehigh County."

The woman, Candice Spahn, was the mother of then-five-year-old Ashley Spahn, who had autism. After the alarming incidents, she had called a local police department to inquire about PLI, but the person "proceeded to put down Project Lifesaver, told her it was 'worthless,' 'don't do it,' 'it's a waste of money,'" Lieberman said. "You name it, and this police department told her this.

"Somehow she got my name," Lieberman continued, "and she called me. And I went through the roof. When she started telling me this, I really planted my heels and said 'this isn't going to work. We're going to get this program going again.'"

Lieberman pitched the family's story to Koltnow as an example of the importance and relevance of Project Lifesaver to citizens. A TV news segment ensued in May 2013.

In October 2014, a year after stepping into her mother's seemingly unfillable shoes, Lieberman achieved a milestone with the placement of the first bracelets in Allentown and Bethlehem police departments' resurrection of PLI since they'd dropped the program in 2009.

Spahn had also played a role in the achievement, Lieberman said. "Because of her family, Allentown and Bethlehem police departments got back into the program and got their training. And because I wasn't going to take *no* for an answer," she added. "Nobody was going to tell me that this program was horrible. And they were not going to tell me that this child's life was going to be in danger because they don't think it's worth the program."

By the year's end, the news of Allentown and Bethlehem resuming Project Lifesaver, and of Lower Milford PD's plan to start, had been publicly announced. That success represented victory for what Lieberman and her mother had been trying for years to accomplish, but it didn't guarantee knockout triumph in Lieberman's own continuous fight. Round X had only begun, albeit charged by this new momentum. And she stood firmer, more diligent and more relentless backed by increasing public awareness and demand.

Still, it wasn't easy.

"There was a lot of talking with people, going to meetings, and building up Project Lifesaver again," Lieberman said. "It was a hard task." People don't always see the need, and some tend to put a negative spin on anything not proven directly to them, she explained. "But I had an impossible dream," she said. "I was going to get it going. So I fought, and I spoke to people, and I fought some more."

Lieberman's efforts continued to raise awareness, but not in time for everyone who needed it.

On New Year's Eve 2015, five-year-old Jayliel Vega Batista wandered into the night from a family house party in Allentown. According to news reports, a two-day search for the autistic child involved Allentown police and firefighters, local volunteers, about twenty dogs, three helicopters, and eleven search-and-rescue teams from other parts of the state as well as from New Jersey and New York and others.

"Over a thousand people searched for this little boy," Lieberman said. They had hoped the barefoot child who had left without a coat had found shelter someplace where he could still be found safe—perhaps beneath a porch or in a car.

Instead, Jayliel's body was found January 2, 2016, in the nearby Lehigh Canal.

"I thought, *no, this cannot be,*" Lieberman said. "And I started working even harder. And I went to town hall meetings, and I went to borough meetings. And I went to every meeting you could possibly think of. I said, 'This is Project Lifesaver, and this is why you need it.'"

Jayliel's mother, Yelitza Batista, later requested that Lieberman speak during an autism-awareness program. Lieberman did, and the two women joined in the commitment to protect other vulnerable citizens of Lehigh Valley.

According to Lieberman, because of Jayliel and the publicity surrounding the tragedy, the mayor, police department and other organizations donated thirty-nine bracelets to Allentown's Project Lifesaver program. A local hospital funded the program for an additional police department. "And the word got around that Jayliel is still with us," she said. "He has become the voice of autism in our area. And it's just unfortunate that it took his dying to bring it to life."

One might expect that such a grave cost would command widespread engagement.

Not necessarily so.

"Still to this day, it's been a very hard struggle," Lieberman said, adding that she sometimes attends meetings and events as many as five days a week. She embraces every opportunity to promote PLI, including her ability to organize commemorative events, press conferences and ongoing media relations with Koltnow and others. "But sometimes you have to go a little bit further," she said, "and I did. Sometimes an extreme measure is needed, but you have to know where to stop."

Immediately following local searches, she approaches the public-safety agencies, assisted-living homes and other entities associated with the incidents or in a position to help mitigate future events. "I say, 'We've got to do this; *this* is the *reason* that we have to do this,'" she reiterated.

On that note, she referenced a single Lehigh County town that had recently had two Alzheimer's patients wander in the same week. She had pressed local officials and agencies: *This is why you need this program, so this doesn't happen again.*

She cited another two patients who had recently wandered in Northampton County. "I was able to walk in and say, 'Look, this is your back door. You need this,'" she said.

And a woman in Salisbury had been missing for about a week, having strayed from a nursing home. Upon Lieberman's return home from the conference, she planned to visit that facility with the same message. Unfortunately, she would learn that the missing woman had not survived.

Over the years, Lieberman has learned how far she can push while remaining in line with rules and regulations. Just as Saunders had experienced in his own career, people *hem* and *haw* and make excuses for why they don't deem the program necessary or why it won't work. Yet as often as she outlines the savings in terms of human lives, time and taxpayer resources, "people don't want to hear it," she said.

But like Saunders', Lieberman's spirit won't be undermined by naysayers. "It just makes me angrier," she said of the apathy. "And it makes me really want to push that much further. Project Lifesaver has a recovery time of half an hour or less, as compared to hours, days or longer for searches that don't always deliver the same positive result. The equipment makes it so much easier to locate a person. And in my eyes the primary benefit would be the satisfaction they receive by locating someone and bringing them home safe.

"It's a no-brainer," Lieberman insisted. "But they don't get it. And short of hitting them over the head, I don't know what else to do," she half-joked.

"Now that's something I got from my mother," she conceded. "She made quite an impression within Project Lifesaver and on the people in our area. And I did learn from her: *You don't give up.*

"It's a tribute to her," Lieberman said of taking the reins. She looked at the image of the cane on the presentation screen.

"People say that Moses parted the Red Sea with his staff," she continued. "Well, Judith Lieberman conquered Lehigh County with her cane. And that cane stood for something in Lehigh County. To this day, people remember that cane and they remember her.

"She never hit anybody over the head, although she threatened to." Lieberman laughed. "She never beat anybody with it. But she became known" for her passion, determination and perseverance— and for the cane that ominously preceded her tireless steps toward progress. "I don't use it," she said of the well-worn and -weathered keepsake, "but it's on the top shelf of a bookcase, where, appropriately, I have to look up to see it."

Lieberman continues the good fight. Compensation for her own volunteer effort arrives in the form of internal reward. "I believe in this program so much," she said. "I do it because it's the thing to do. I'm doing this for free, but it's not for free. Because I'm getting the satisfaction, knowing that I'm doing something."

It's a long battle, she assured. "You have to keep promoting. You have to keep going out and talking up the program and explaining to people, over and over again sometimes, what the program is and why it's needed," she urged. "Use examples. That's what's needed sometimes. That's the only way to get through to some people. Just take that cane and hit 'em over the head if you have to."

"I do things my way," Lieberman said. "And I will continue to do things my way. And you know what?" she posed. "We're getting there, which makes me feel great."

By the end of 2018, the official Project Lifesaver International agency count for Lehigh Valley was seventeen. "It's all about tenacity," Lieberman concluded. "Don't give up."

WHAT CARETAKERS AND OTHERS NEED TO UNDERSTAND

Lieberman's story speaks volumes, Saunders said. On a community level, one of the biggest challenges Saunders still faces is helping caretakers, public-safety agents and others to understand the importance of the Project Lifesaver program, the value it delivers on multiple levels, and what successful implementation actually entails.

The initial hurdle often involves overcoming caretakers' deniability of the problem. The first time a person wanders, it's easy for guardians to argue that he or she has only wandered once, Saunders said. "Well," he poses, "how many times do you want them to do it?"

Others argue that their loved ones only wander within the neighborhood. Saunders asks, "What will happen the day the neighbors don't spot them?"

To caretakers who presume their wanderer won't wear a device, Saunders asks, simply, "How do you know?" And for those participants who do refuse a wrist bracelet, he'll find some other way—maybe strap it to the ankle. Trained PLI agents can even desensitize a reluctant child by pre-exposing him or her to the bracelet for short periods of time until it no longer feels alien to the wearer.

Coming from another perspective, parents worry about stigma. They don't want their children to be singled out or identified by others as "different," Saunders explained. He reminds these parents that a lot of people wear jewelry and adornments of all sorts. While the tracking bracelets are relatively unobtrusive, they can also be dressed up to look more like accessories. Parents need to weigh the pros and cons, he said. On behalf of a child prone to running away or wandering, which is the utmost concern: suiting him with a device that might save his life, or the chance that someone irrelevant might remark about it?

Nor does the equipment monitor a participant 24/7, Saunders often assures privacy-minded patients and guardians. "It's not Big Brother watching," he explained. "The only time that it's even in use is if they go missing. And then we'll come in and start locating the radio signal and tracking to it. But it's not like we know where they are twenty-four hours a day or have some kind of hold on them," he said. Furthermore, the service is only provided within a voluntary context, that is, either the participant or a caregiver with legal authority requests it. "And I've had Alzheimer's patients tell me themselves, 'I'm moving into this stage, and I need it,'" Saunders said.

EQUIPMENT AND TECHNOLOGY CLARIFICATIONS

The next challenge is to clarify the differences in available technologies, what may best suit a particular situation and why, and what might be problematic or not work at all in a specific locale.

"We need to explain to clients what will work, what won't; when GPS will work very well for them and when it will not; when radio frequency (RF) is the best solution; and why we do it through police and public-safety departments as opposed to wanting to leave it completely with loved ones," Saunders elaborated.

While the individual needs and logistical specifications of clients call for general variety in equipment offerings, technologies other than radio-frequency identification (RF/RFID) serve only as secondary and in concert with RF, which has proven the most reliable and accurate for Project Lifesaver purposes.

"We really rely on this, and we come right back to it," Carter affirmed. "It's basic, and it doesn't require anything else to work." Cell phone technologies require towers, he said; GPS relies on satellites. The reliability of each is conditional, depending upon multiple variables. "RF supports itself."

Carter and Saunders often find themselves correcting the misperception that in this world of technological advancements, people can slap a GPS on someone and know where they are twenty-four hours a day, even if they're five stories below ground, behind a boiler. "That's not exactly true," Saunders said.

Radio frequency signals are more direct and work in places that cell and GPS technologies don't, Carter reiterated, driving home the leading advantage of PLI's primary tracking methodology. Even in optimal environments, neither cell nor GPS application can pinpoint a location as spot-on as RF can. "When you cut that on and dial in a frequency, it's looking for that exact transmitter that somebody's wearing," he explained.

"And you don't know where you're going to find them," Carter continued. PLI clients have been found in basements, closets, even hidden inside a doghouse and stowed away inside a drop-ceiling. "They'll go and get themselves mired up someplace where you're not going to get signals from cell phones and other technologies," he said. What's more, the RF transmitters in current usage are highly water-resistant, and their signals have been tested and detected from as deep as twelve feet underwater.

The ancillary technologies can enhance the PLI experience for some clients, Saunders said, "but we're very careful when people call us and inquire about it," he noted. It's important that folks understand that PLI is a nonprofit organization, not one of the for-profit businesses offering similar-sounding alternatives.

Terminology used by others can be confusing, Saunders said. For example, some analogue equipment is "digitally tuned," he explained. "Well, that doesn't mean anything," he said. "That only means that you took an analogue box, you hooked it up to your digital tuner, you got it tuned, and then you unplugged it. But it's still analogue. It does not change the function or the operation," he said; the difference between a digital tracker and an analogue tracker is "still night and day."

Most people don't understand the technical nuances. "This is one of many reasons that I tell everyone here, 'When you answer a call or an inquiry about alternative technology, such as GPS, make sure that these people understand what it is and how it's used,'" Saunders continued, "rather than, 'OK, how many do you want, how soon do you need it, and here it is,' with no regard as to whether it's going to work in their area, whether they're going to understand it or it's even going to be of any benefit to them," he said. Instead, ask about their cell-phone coverage or other applicable variables, "and predetermine that it has a good chance of being successful before we ever let them have it."

In fact, Project Lifesaver's RF technology itself presents alternatives that may suit those inquirers better than other technologies would, Saunders said. For instance, in communities that don't yet have the program, caretakers can order tracking units, transmitters and instructional videos directly from PLI, and individually manage the equipment and monitoring. It's a limited recommendation, only for those who don't have access to PLI, Saunders warned. It generally does not apply to caretakers who simply express a *preference* for that option, because foregoing the first-responder expertise can work against them come search time. "Many loved ones in these situations become so emotionally involved and stressed that anything we've trained them to do can go right out the window," Saunders explained. "But public-safety people are trained to react in emergencies. They're trained to perform. They're trained to get past the emotional and personal aspect of it and work on the functionality and the location and locating the signal, and if there's a problem, they're trained in how to deal with it, get around it and find a solution rather than going to pieces emotionally."

OBSERVATIONS AND INTERACTIONS

But caretakers do play crucial roles in other ways. The importance of their observations prior to a wandering incident cannot be overstated, and their recollections of communications and mindsets involving their loved ones or patients can prove invaluable. When first responders arrive on scene, they need all the insight they can get.

"One of the things that we had found, once we'd really gotten into this, was that we could almost predict when somebody was going to go," Saunders said. "And we would tell the caregivers at the start to pay attention to what they're saying, pay attention to when they say they need to go somewhere or they need to be somewhere or they want to go home.

"Now, they may *be* home, but not in their mind," he explained. "Because their home in their mind at that point may be twenty years in the past. So where was their mind at the time? What were they talking about? Did they make reference to anybody within a certain time frame? You know, like 'Uncle Bob.' Well, Uncle Bob's been dead for twenty years. OK, we assume they're thinking back at least twenty years now. Where was home twenty years ago?

"So pay attention to those kinds of things," he urges. "What were they talking about? What was their interest? What was their focus . . . because that is a prelude, quite often, that they are getting restless, they are getting ready to go, they have *developed a mission*," as Saunders recalled coining the term prior to it catching on elsewhere. "They have a mission," he explained. "What is that mission? They're going home? They're going to pick up the kids? They're going to work?"

While this information isn't always the key, it's often very helpful in terms of predicting when someone might be intent on wandering off, or in which direction he or she might have already set out. Saunders again recalled the man from Western Branch: "He was on a straight line to his old workplace. . . . And he didn't make it."

As if life for hard-working caregivers isn't stressful enough, some dementia sufferers also develop sundown syndrome, getting their days and nights mixed up and becoming recharged, restless and ready for the day in late-afternoon or evening. By then, caregivers would typically be winding down. Additional symptoms can include anxiousness, confusion, irritability, delirium and other hard-to-handle behaviors that can tax overwhelmed caretakers to the point of complete exhaustion. During the very hours when they should be getting restorative sleep, their escape-prone loved ones may be most in need of a watchful eye.

BROADENING PERSPECTIVES

Once a person with cognitive disorders goes missing, the vulnerabilities start to stack up. One source of their susceptibility that's often overlooked is ignorance—on the part of the public.

Upon meeting Bob Smith for the first time, anyone unfamiliar with the visual and behavioral subtleties in his seemingly neurotypical appearance could easily miss the fact that he's autistic and instead misjudge his state of mind or intentions. Untrained law-enforcement agents are no exception.

Smith's mom, Gayle Schultz, recalled another two of the "big events" at the forefront of her many memories of her son's distressing adventures:

Norfolk to Virginia Beach, twice trouble

In 2004, following his traumatizing overnight bike ride the previous year, Smith had moved back in with the Schultzes. They lived in Norfolk, and Smith had a bedroom of his own.

The household and its routines changed abruptly when Schultz's mom, who could no longer reside independently due to Alzheimer's disease, moved in as well, and Schultz's brother arrived for an extended visit.

"Bob didn't really like that," Schultz recalled. To him, the lifestyle restructuring represented chaos.

Smith gathered his backpack and took off on his bike again, this time with hurt feelings and a secret agenda. As snow pelted the ground and the temperature hovered around nineteen degrees, he cycled from his home in Norfolk to a church miles away in Virginia Beach. There he told the youth pastor that he had no place to go, no family in the area, and he was ready to get a job and start a new life.

The youth pastor, having no reason to doubt the young man in need, offered Smith a temporary home with him while Smith searched for work.

"But all those apartments looked the same," Schultz recalled. And upon returning to the complex from one of his job hunts, "Bob tried to get into the wrong apartment. He was knocking on some lady's door, saying, 'Let me in! Let me in! Let me in!' And she called the police," presuming malice.

Meanwhile, "we were in a panic, unable to find him," Schultz said.

But Smith had become a Project Lifesaver client after his bike-in-the-rain adventure the previous year, and multiple facets of the program had already been set in motion this time.

"Finally, we get a call from Virginia Beach police," Schultz continued. "They said, 'We have your son in custody,' and I'm thinking, *Oh, my gosh; what do you mean in custody?* They said, 'He's in the car. We think it's your son. He refuses to give us his name or even say anything to us.'"

Schultz wasn't surprised. Her son's past experiences with police had been at best defensive and tense and at worst quite troubling.

"Several times in his life, just because he seemed different, he's been harassed by police while walking down the street," she explained. "Because Bob will do interesting things, like wear sunglasses at night" or decline to show identification. "So immediately the police think, *What's wrong with this guy? What's up with him?*"

She recalled a day when officers approached Smith as he tried to catch a bus at five a.m. He wore a favorite hooded sweatshirt and had lost his pants belt. "So he was walking around, wearing a hoodie because it was cold, pulling his pants up, wearing his sunglasses, catching the bus," she said. "And they stopped him and harassed him because he looked suspicious."

Barring harassment, these were perfect examples of how the critical and generally advantageous *situational awareness* to which Saunders refers can misfire if applied to an innocent member of the community and carried too far due to misunderstanding.

And so when Virginia Beach police called Schultz after Smith had taken off with his bike again in 2004, during the extreme winter weather, she felt both relief and angst. Her son was safe, but handcuffed and detained. He must have been terrified. The officers said they would have arrested him if not for an all-points bulletin that had conveyed the special circumstances and led them to her.

That APB was one component of the Project Lifesaver program operating out of Norfolk Sheriff's Office and coordinated by Paul Ballance. Agents had begun working with local police departments as soon as Schultz had reported Smith missing.

Numerous subsequent incidents were resolved quickly, thanks to PLI, before the worst of what Schultz refers to as the "big events" during a heat wave in July 2011: Smith had gotten up early, as usual, and without telling anyone caught a bus from Norfolk to a residential community at the Virginia Beach oceanfront. When Schultz noticed him missing, she called Ballance.

"These guys are amazing," Schultz said of the team. "They get out, no matter what time you call them. They call their posse, and they are *out* and *about* searching."

The ground search began with the area near Smith's home. Meanwhile PLI agents and volunteers launched what would become a full-out, collaborative, intercity public-awareness campaign, notifying local news outlets, police and rescue departments and transit agencies; blowing up social media; faxing and posting flyers wherever they thought might be relevant; and anything else they could do.

While the specialized tracking equipment system is a primary arm of Project Lifesaver International's total deployment, these ancillary tactics held the key this time. Smith had travelled so far, and gotten such a head start outside the range of expectations and electronic signal detection, but members of the public-safety and civilian sects throughout surrounding cities were on the lookout.

"It was an all-out manhunt for Bob," Schultz said. "I mean, we had it going on. We were not playing. Because it was too hot for Bob to be anywhere by himself with no resources."

On day three, a woman reported having found Smith. She recognized him from a flyer she had seen in a bakery the day before. He was sitting under a tree outside a store.

"Everyone was relieved," Schultz recalled, "and it starts with Project Lifesaver. They get the ball rolling. With Project Lifesaver, force mobilization is instantaneous."

Her son had been found exhausted, dehydrated, sunburned and blistered, having gotten lost and been wandering for two days trying to find his way home. "He had asked people for help," Schultz said, "but they told him 'No.' They just thought he was a homeless person."

Schultz later learned that one night her son had slept on a park bench. Teens playing basketball approached him, harassed him and threatened to kick his ass, he told her.

It's pathetic, infuriating, Schultz lamented. "I mean, what kind of society do you live in when you can see that someone has special needs and nobody says, 'Hey, I have a phone. Can I call somebody for you?'"

Malevolence aside, much of the problem boils down to lack of awareness, Ballance said. People are simply not in the habit of attempting to distinguish troublemakers from individuals with cognitive disorders. And in cases like Smith's, individuals can appear suspicious because their abnormal behavior does not align with how otherwise "normal" they look.

The need for enlightenment clearly extends to law-enforcement, Saunders said. "I think cops, if they've been in it long enough—and the majority of them don't even think about it—but they do automatic threat assessment," he explained. "When they see a person, they're automatically assessing: *Is this person a threat? Is this situation threatening?* They develop 'the vibes,' the feelings. You know, *wait a minute, something's not right here. Pay attention to it.*"

It comes with the LEO territory, but "there have been too many situations where somebody with special needs or a behavioral disorder has been misjudged and it led to tragic results," Saunders said. "Yes, a law-enforcement officer has to think about his or her safety, but they also need to be able to recognize *what are we dealing with here*, and then look for the clues."

And Smith's situation is one example that represents an array of profound challenges for countless others like him.

Lieberman concurs. She referenced a young autistic man in Salisbury, Pennsylvania, who had wandered from his family's car in summer 2017. "Twenty years old, six-feet-something, and about 230 pounds," she noted. "My main concern was that he looks 'normal,' and somebody's going to say something, and he's going to fly off the handle. And what's going to happen? The police will be called." On one hand, that would be a good thing because he would have been located, she said, but on the other hand was the real potential for unnecessary trauma, injury or worse, "because people don't understand autism at all."

"Law enforcement needs to understand how to recognize and interact with these persons," Saunders affirmed. "This is one of the reasons why the hallmark of our trainings is just that."

Project Lifesaver training has three main components. They address search patterns, operating and troubleshooting equipment, and how to perceptively and effectively approach and interact with the subjects once found.

"Half the battle is finding the subject," Carter noted. "The other half is interacting with them. You can have a bad time, or it'll go smoothly and you can take them home without an incident."

An "incident" can involve risk to either party. Agents need to know how to keep everyone safe, including themselves. It's not uncommon for a subject to turn on somebody attempting to assist him or her due to fear, emotional distress or general cognitive disorientation, Saunders said. "When I first started, I had a retired Airforce officer who at one time had been a Golden Gloves boxer," he recalled. "Well, don't you know I really danced around when I had to go up and approach *him*!"

For Norfolk's Paul Ballance, working with PLI has been a "life-changer" to that end. He'd thought he'd seen it all in twenty-five years with the fire department, but his involvement with PLI at the sheriff's office has awakened him to the challenges of people with cognitive disorders, and adjusted his attitude toward some of the behaviors he sees in public. "That child acting out in a mall," for instance, "might not be a product of 'poor parenting' but might be a child on the autism spectrum," he said. "That elderly person talking to himself on the street corner might not be 'crazy' but have a mild form of dementia."

So, what signs might indicate the difference?

"Unless it's something such as Down syndrome, or some other disorder that has a physical characteristic, you probably won't know," Saunders said. "And yes, sometimes the behavior can appear suspicious." He advises civilians not to approach the unfamiliar person directly if they don't know what they're doing. "Instead," he said, "go ahead and call law-enforcement."

Officers can then look for clues, such as locator devices or ID bracelets, or how the individual responds to an interaction.

For example, "When you do approach them and start talking, how are they responding to you?" he posed. "Many autistic children, or even teenagers or adults, won't look you in the eye when they're talking to you." That's a behavior commonly associated with lying, but it could in fact indicate another problem, he explained. "Then, after you engage them for a couple of minutes, just like recognizing an elderly person with Alzheimer's, you need to understand *how* to interact and talk to them, how to gauge if there's a problem. And then, what kind of conversation do you engage them in?"

It's always a fact-finding mission, but you have to know how the facts add up, Saunders said. "There've been situations where a law enforcement officer has stopped Alzheimer's patients who were driving vehicles and asked them the standard questions, and the people were able to respond logically, and they let them go," he explained. "And they ended up not being found ever again, or found dead.

"Was that the officer's fault?" he asked. "No. The problem was that the officer did not know how to recognize indicators or engage that person in order to figure out there's more of a problem here."

It happens all the time, hence the importance of widespread, ongoing training on the subject, to both existing and new-coming LEOs. Saunders cited examples of common scenarios and the type of more-effective response he puts forth in PLI training. For instance, an Alzheimer's patient, when asked to show his driver's license and registration, may have them. Prodding deeper begets more insight, Saunders explained, suggesting dialogue of the following sort:

"'Where are you going?'

"'I'm going home.'

"'Well, where is home?' . . . 'OK, is that the address that's on this license?' . . . 'That's not the address that's on this license. Can you tell me the difference?'

"What you'll begin to find out," Saunders explained, "is that they can't put all that together logically—'Where are you coming from? Is there anyone I can call?' You know, those kinds of things.

"If you want a trivial answer, use very simple questions," he said. "But if you really want to find out if they can comprehend and engage, use a complex question: 'What time did you leave home, where are you going, and when are you supposed to be back?'

"They can't filter that," he said. "So now, there's a problem. Now you start to recognize, *OK, we have more than just a traffic violation here. Or we have more than just a shoplifting violation. Or we have more than just somebody standing around watching people or wandering up and down the sidewalk.*

"The same with an autistic child or a child with some other disorder," he continued. "It's about learning to recognize, in conversation, some of the physical or mental characteristics they are going to demonstrate—such as getting very upset, or wanting to touch you. Or what they call *echolalia*, where you ask them a question and they repeat it back to you. Or not talking at all, not answering, not looking you in the eye," he said. "Those are some kinds of signals that indicate there needs a little bit more follow-up here than just the standard 'Who are you? Where are you going? Give me some identification.'

"It's awareness, you know," and every cop should have it, Saunders said. "Just because you're vice, or narcotics, or tactical, or SWAT, doesn't mean that out here on the streets you're not going to run across these people," he forewarned. "Let's say you get a dementia patient who barricades himself," he proposed. "OK, now you're thinking, *I wish I'd have known something about how to handle this. I wish I'd have known how to interact with them. I wish I'd have known how they think.*

"Well, why wait until then?" he urged. "Prepare yourself. If you're going to be a good law-enforcement officer or a good law-enforcement agency, you're going to look at what is happening around you, not only in your community but all around you," elsewhere nationwide, he said. "What is happening with the day-to-day policing, the stuff on the street? Are people running into more autistic kids? Alzheimer's patients? Dementia patients? And what have been the outcomes?"

GETTING BEHIND THE MOVEMENT

According to Paul Ballance, as of autumn 2016, Norfolk Sheriff's Office had responded to more than 350 service calls for its PLI clients since Sheriff Bob McCabe first integrated the program in 2001. Ballance said his passion for Project Lifesaver grows daily, with every family member he meets, because few things in life compare with witnessing and participating in the saving of lives of people who cannot help themselves. Agents throughout North America echo the sentiment year after year.

But while individual agents may recognize the importance and advantages of the Project Lifesaver model, it's not always easy getting past the shortsightedness of some of their administrators.

"They don't all feel there's a need for it," Saunders said. For whatever reason, "some won't recognize that there's a problem in their community and that whether they like it or not, they are the first line. And there are police administrators out there who still think that police work is 'us against the crooks.' They only do community service things because they're absolutely forced to. But policing is not that anymore," he said; that notion is obsolete. "It's not the 'us against the crooks' reality; that's only part of it.

"They've got to understand that there are other things going on in the community, and like it or not, they are going to end up dealing with these things," Saunders assured. "So you might as well be proactive in your dealing," he urged, based upon his own labyrinthine experience. "Just saying, 'Well, I don't have a wandering problem,' yet you're going out on two or three searches a month" doesn't make sense, he said. Even in a year's time, "a lot of them say, 'Well, we had two. So it's not a big deal.'"

With that, Saunders challenges them: "You don't have a problem?" he'll pose. "How much time did you spend looking for those people? And what were the results?" If the events were typical, "then you've got a problem," he'll conclude. "And you need to deal with it." And when they say they've never had one, his antennae go up.

Sure, "you can play ostrich all you want," Saunders said; "stick your head in the sand, and if I don't see it or hear it, it doesn't exist; but that doesn't work anymore. It just doesn't."

With that said, for all of Saunders' mission-driven sense, he can still put himself in the slow-comers' shoes.

"In another sense," he reasoned, "I understand that this is only one thing they deal with. You know, there are so many things out there that, for lack of an alternative responsive agency, it all falls into law enforcement's lap." He sympathizes. "Let's face it: if anything happens out there, regardless of what it is, who gets called? The cops; law enforcement," he said. "And unfortunately, all of these things that are going on in our society are not going away. So you need to address them.

"So I know they have to build their priorities," Saunders affirmed. "But *this* is becoming more and more of a priority."

Why? "First off," Saunders said, "look at the time and manpower that is allocated to these types of situations." Standard searches typically start small, and as time passes they grow exponentially. The nearly two-week-long Western Branch search cost taxpayers about

$340,000-plus, he said, "and then for it to be a failure made it worse. And you're pulling from other things that you should be doing in order to search for this person, whereas if you had a program such as Project Lifesaver, where you could locate them in 20 or 30 minutes with two or three agents, it's done, it's over, you move on," he said.

"Secondly, you're being proactive in the community," he continued. "And let's face it: Any time the community feels like you're doing something to help them, that goes over in a positive manner." Familiarity with the kind and assistive nature of officers, who are human members of society no different from the civilian public, can help offset the imbalance weighted by the negative nature of the job. "So if you need support from the community someday, they're more apt to respond to you in a positive way rather than, 'What have you done for the community except put people in jail?'" he explained.

Carter and Ballance concurred with Saunders' points.

It's irrefutable that nothing compares to the effectiveness and expediency of PLI in the time-sensitive push to prevent tragedy, Ballance said. "Thanks to Gene's vision and continued dedication, an average search is thirty minutes with Project Lifesaver technology," he said, and time is money. On traditional searches, "the man-hours and taxpayers' money spent are astronomical."

Carter elaborated: For the cost of a single typical standard search, about $13,500, two to three Project Lifesaver agencies could be established. "And that's a renewable resource," he said. For $5,000 or less, an agency gets set up, correctly trained, and furnished with equipment that is reusable, search after search, year after year. Even the equipment is backward-compatible, which means that new equipment doesn't render existing equipment obsolete. Upgrades and additions to the line are based upon agent feedback and designed or selected to work with existing equipment, avoiding the need for agencies to spend money on unnecessarily replacing perfectly good stock. Most importantly, he added, consider the mortal value of every *successful* search.

Furthermore, police and sheriffs' departments don't have to bear the brunt; they're not the only appropriate member-agency prospects, Carter said. Assisted-living facilities, VA hospitals, fire and rescue departments and myriad other health-care and public-safety organizations fit the ideal PLI profile. Think outside the box.

As for public relations, Carter noted that PLI agents who develop relationships with their clients are building community rapport. They represent their departments as agents of good will through ongoing friendly interactions facilitated by such simple occurrences as routine visits for battery changes.

"It's a community-relations tool for law enforcement," he said. "You're going out to visit a family, and it's a good thing," a positive event vs. a crisis response. It can break the isolation that caretakers often experience, and it offers the opportunity for agents to share helpful circumstantial insights. They're also laying potentially vital groundwork for future searches, he noted. The clients come to recognize and trust the agents during these lower-stress interactions, and then, during high-stress search-and-rescue scenarios, the lost may have enough instinctual memory to approach an agent or accept assistance when approached.

The decision-makers whom Saunders has the least trouble convincing, the ones who come to PLI most quickly and readily, are those who are in the executive hierarchy and are aware of all the pluses, Saunders said. They know the challenges and know the potential of PLI. "They're the ones who have dealt with the issue and lost somebody because they didn't find them quickly enough or they still haven't found them," he noted. "That's a real eye-opener for some police executives."

Yet, some agencies that clearly recognize the need for PLI in their communities remain stumped at the level of resource acquisition and management. They argue that while they see the value, they still lack the money and the manpower to initiate and operate the program.

In other words, they have the sense of *purpose* but what they really lack is the refinement of other key elements: *vision*, *determination* and *tenacity*. Fortunately, Saunders and other Project Lifesaver champions have more than enough to share.

"Funding is a major issue," Lieberman affirmed. To assist the Lehigh Valley community, she sponsors fundraisers, helps agencies pursue grants, asks for donations, appeals to local and state elected officials, and continues to speak to groups that help spread the word and might also produce a philanthropic gift of equipment or cash. She recalled a few good examples of success.

"There was one very small town, Emmaus, and they told me

'It's not going to happen,' they don't have the money, they're never going to get the money," Lieberman said. "So I sponsored a garage sale, and we raised some funds. But we didn't raise enough. So what happened? Somebody donated $5,000, sponsored Emmaus. Emmaus is now a participating member of Project Lifesaver."

Lieberman had also been working since 2013 to get state funding. In July 2017, Sen. Patrick Browne gave her permission to declare a breakthrough at the Project Lifesaver annual conference the following month: "Gene," she announced, "this one's for you. We are guaranteed $100,000 from the state." Through the applause, she continued: "The money is ours. He's found money, through a line item . . . and it's going to be a pilot program for Lehigh County."

Saunders was thrilled. But he'd had to work with Lieberman and the Commonwealth of Pennsylvania to make it happen, he said. For example, he explained, "one of the problems they had was, 'How do we get the money out there?'" The solution was easy: "Being a 501(c)(3), we can manage the money for nonprofits and government money," he said. "So the way the pilot will work is that the money will be sent to Project Lifesaver, we will manage it and report back to the Commonwealth of Pennsylvania where it goes, who has it, and what the results are. And we're more than willing to do that for others."

PLI has been helping agencies in similar ways for years, including police departments that have trouble raising money and keeping it.

"One of the problems is, and we experienced this years ago," Saunders explained, "that when some have raised money, and they put it into the city coffers, what did the city manager do when he saw it in there? He took it; he said, 'No, that's city money.' So a lot of police departments now will raise the money and send it to us, and we will establish an account for them. So if they want to purchase equipment or do anything in their Project Lifesaver program, we will have it there, they can come back to us, and we will send them whatever they need, or we will take equipment calls out of that, and we will continually give them an accounting of the funds that they have in there." In other cases, the departments ask that donations be sent directly to Project Lifesaver where they are earmarked for the agency via a fiduciary fund.

Saunders would love to give the equipment away, he said in 2018, "but the manufacturers don't give it to me. And the power and light companies don't give me power and light, and the telephone people don't give me phone services." As a nonprofit, PLI stretches is current annual budget of approximately $950,000 as far as it can. And part of the value of being a nonprofit is the ability to pursue grants and other avenues for funding, in order to keep the program as affordable as possible to members, Saunders said. As a nonprofit, "we don't have to worry about making a profit, or being able to pay dividends to investors, and worry if I'm making enough money that I can be rich and comfortable. That's not what we're in it for."

Saunders also encourages partnering with others of like-cause and like-mission within the community to help alleviate the burden of sole responsibility. For instance, many PLI agencies have agents go to clients' homes to change wristband batteries. For those that don't have the manpower, he suggests other ideas. "Get volunteers to do it; maybe you have a senior program, or an auxiliary program. Or maybe you want to pair with a nonprofit organization," he said. "They can take care of the administrative side of the house, including changing batteries and bands if that's what they want, and the PLI agencies will be the responders."

Saunders cited an example in North Carolina: "The sheriff did not have the means to do the program, but there was a nursing home that did," he said. "So this nonprofit nursing home jumped in there and said 'We can do this.' The nursing home brought the program into their facility and included the sheriff's department. So now the sheriff is a backup for that nursing home but also does it for the rest of the county. So it worked out very well."

Partnerships also create new, cooperative, and mutually beneficial opportunities for cross-promotion and raising awareness of complementary missions.

Some fire departments have gotten innovative in another way, inviting clients to the station once or twice a month and making it a big party. People come in, they see the fire trucks, they get batteries and bands changed, and it's become a fun and positive community event.

"Of course, agencies are always strapped for money and manpower," Carter said, "because their budgets are always getting slashed." In response to this perennial challenge, PLI offers several other options, including a transmitter that can be programmed for the battery to last sixty days instead of thirty, saving the agency the monetary and human resources involved in the standard maintenance. Alternatively, caregivers may lease transmitters directly from PLI and have them delivered to their local PLI agencies for proper installation, relieving those agencies of the money-handling and administrative barrier. And in locales where an agency can't or won't be involved with battery and band maintenance, PLI sends those directly to the caregivers.

The solution variations among approximately 1,600 PLI agencies today run the gamut, Saunders said, "and every community has its own personality, its own way of doing things. Anything we can do to make a program work, make it easier for members, we're going to do it. Where there's a will, there's a way."

Once an agency has decided to implement Project Lifesaver, the leadership will be key, Saunders said.

"If you're going to address this issue, make sure that whomever you put in charge of it is somebody who cares," he urges. "It's like anything else: If somebody cares about something, they're going to do it and do it well. If they don't care, if this guy has no more interest in doing it than the man in the moon, well, what kind of service or response are you going to get? Probably none or very little," he said; "it's just something else they will get to when they get the chance. And I've seen it, so I know it happens."

Good leadership extends to the realm of promotion, and Project Lifesaver spends only scant amounts on paid advertising—primarily with cause-related trade publications. All else is organic promotion, and Carter noted the longstanding proven effectiveness of this—not only in terms of cost, but more importantly in terms of the value of the trust and authenticity that continue to inspire countless walking, talking spokespeople.

"The good thing about Project Lifesaver is that we rely on our own reputation," he said. "It's all word of mouth. Agencies talk to agencies." He sees it happen at conferences year-round, he said: Sheriffs unfamiliar with PLI come to the Project Lifesaver table and ask questions, and another sheriff who has PLI will come over and talk up the program and tell them they need it. Other effective means include social media and the positive illumination resulting from many years' worth of earned traditional media coverage.

The promotion must be ongoing, Lieberman affirmed. Even after an agency has funded establishment and operations, "you're always going to need the money to keep the program going," she said. "So that means you have to keep talking to the right people," including members of the media, state and local government officials and groups that can help broaden awareness and help raise funds.

And don't be afraid to get tough when necessary. When she's up against bureaucratic resistance, "I go and I argue," Lieberman said. "Politely, sometimes, but I argue."

Despite the tremendous value of this grass-roots methodology, PLI's organic promotion must compete with the more widespread attention garnered by other causes and organizations, such as those related to cancer research and awareness. Those with larger budgets can afford to spend money on advertising. When it comes time to give, Saunders urges people to consider not only those causes with which they're most familiar, but also the plight of people with cognitive disorders and the life-saving value of PLI.

"There are a lot of things out there that are society woes, and I understand and have no problem with the big push for some of these other causes," Saunders said. "And I understand that if something affects you, you have more passion for it.

"But I think that when it comes to autism, dementia and other cognitive disorders, sometimes these get put on the back burner," he said. "Yet when somebody has dementia and they wander, how many people are affected now? You have the family, the neighbors, law enforcement, and anybody who happens upon them." It's a broad societal impact, he explained. "If the police department has to go out and search for them for eight or nine hours, are you affected? Yes, you are." Engaging multiple officers in a search means that incidents elsewhere may lose attention or response time, and that impacts those citizens in need, he noted. "And who pays for that search? You do, as a taxpayer," and at a significantly lower return on that mandatory investment than what Project Lifesaver, fueled by voluntary donations, can deliver, he said.

"Every time somebody wanders, a lot of people get hit in the pocketbook," Saunders reasoned, "so you need to understand the parallel. You need to recognize this as a huge problem. But people just kind of dismiss it. It's not recognized as it should be. So I think people just need to understand that" the initiatives we hear about most often, those that are often top of mind because of surrounding PR, "are not the only things in the world that are happening."

When it comes to promoting the virtues of anything worthy, "it all comes back to standing your ground and fighting for what you believe," Lieberman said. "And everybody's got it in them" to fight.

Saunders agrees wholeheartedly. And the bottom line is this, he said: "If you never give up, anything's attainable."

TWELVE

Technology's Frontier

The autumn sunlight spread across Tommy Carter's desk and onto his office wall in Chesapeake. Life around headquarters had been relatively calm lately. A few feet from Carter sat a coffee cup of water. Immersed inside sat a new Project Lifesaver transmitter. Carter was testing the efficacy of a new high-grade sealant.

"We're always checking these things," he said. "We want to make sure that the equipment is going to perform like it's supposed to perform. That's going to be on somebody whose life depends on it."

All the equipment, no matter the technology, gets tested and approved for use in the field by PLI before it's offered to agencies and clients. Project Lifesaver's aim has always been to be able to grow with technological advancements. The long-standing birds-eye-view vision is flawless because it's simply to do what they need to do to save lives, including changing with whatever technology advancements come their way, Carter explained. They want agencies to have the most up-to-date equipment—tested, tried and approved by PLI.

The most recent—and perhaps most exciting—addition has been that of unmanned aerial vehicle, a.k.a. "drone," technology to the line of PLI's airborne assets. Developed in partnership with Lockheed Martin and Loen Engineering and introduced to the field in 2017, the military-grade PLI Indago UAV is durable, compact and camera-equipped. It enables searches in places where people, cars, helicopters and other traditional delegates cannot always search effectively due to restrictive weather, lighting, terrain and time, among other variables.

Colonel Gary W. Reynolds, Ph.D., retired Lynchburg, Virginia chief of police and former police pilot of fixed-wing aircraft, is now a Project Lifesaver volunteer and assistant. For six years he has taught PLI's Electronic Search Specialist course, teaching agents how to search on the ground. Now, as chief of PLI's UAV operations department, he handles all inquiries about drones and aviation and shares training duties with Saunders. The two men train PLI agents nationwide on drone use in PLI searches.

Neither of the first two rescues by students who he's trained in the method were PLI clients, he said. This makes his case for how broadly relevant the program is, even to wanderers who don't participate in the program.

"One was a ninety-two-year-old hunter," Reynolds recalled. "A helicopter couldn't find him, it was in the mountains, in winter. It got dark, so they called the local sheriff's department to ask them to bring their drone down, and then they marshalled all the searchers and the police helicopter to come back—the mountain was just really dangerous flying," he said. "They were going to start the search again at first light."

But once the sheriff's agents arrived, "it was within something like ten to fifteen minutes that our Project Lifesaver drone found the man and was able to direct the people to bring him out of the woods," Reynolds said. "He had already spent the night with no food or water, a frigid night, and had he spent another night, at age ninety-two and in those conditions, it would have been a different outcome."

The search couldn't have gone more smoothly, Reynolds noted, and the community was lucky to have access to the nearby trained and equipped Project Lifesaver agents. "So now one of the things that I talk about when I'm speaking with either elected officials or law-enforcement executives is the fact that this unit can be used for traditional search-and-rescue in addition to Project Lifesaver," Reynolds said. "So it's a multi-task piece of equipment" with a broad range of applications in any number of possible scenarios.

"There is a tremendous amount of excitement surrounding this," Reynolds said, "and I'm seeing a lot of fire departments interested in this also." Yet not everyone considers the mortal, fiscal and logistical value when considering the cost, he said. "The greatest factor right now, and that's been an Achilles' heel for Project Lifesaver from the beginning, are departments saying they can't afford it," he said. "But our philosophy is, 'You can't afford *not* to have all of this equipment because it serves a purpose of saving lives.'

"That's the obstacle," he continued, "but the reality is that a conventional aircraft can be grounded for maintenance issues or weather, whereas this unit flies in any kind of weather and has very few maintenance issues. A conventional aircraft costs between a half-million to 1.5 million dollars, but you can have this entire unit plus training for $50,000. It costs about $1,000 per hour to operate a helicopter, but the only expense of operating this is whatever the pilot is being paid while on duty, which is not an additional expense," he reasons.

"The weather could be bad, for instance, at the closest airport, and the conventional aircraft could not take off. But you could put this in the trunk of a police car or on a fire truck, drive to the scene if the weather permits, and then launch it from there."

The unit can also be used for mapping a crime scene or disaster assessment, and it's already being used in Florida for storm-damage assessment, navigation and management planning, which benefits police, fire, ambulance, electrical crews and others, Reynolds noted, "so the mission for us is search and rescue, but then it has so many other applications." It's an asset to any locale.

Reynolds makes a great case for value. "Unfortunately," he said, "we are receiving a significant amount of resistance from the public in that they have a fear of either illegal or improper use of the drone by law enforcement. For instance, privacy issues with regard to surveillance line over the property and/or for spying on people in a personal way," he clarified. "And it all really goes back to the Orwellian Big-Brother-type philosophy of government." Reynolds said he can't blame people for that because "it does exist."

The issue is important, Reynolds concedes. "But we know that our mission is very direct, concrete, as to search and rescue, *bringing loved ones home*. Even though the technology has proven to be beneficial with regard to saving lives, and additionally with regard to saving taxpayer money, we still run into barriers from certain members of the public who do not want the police to have this technology. But what is interesting," he countered, "is that the police can already fly over your property in a helicopter or a fixed-wing aircraft. And so the reality is that we're not doing anything that we haven't been doing for decades."

Each state has its own regulations regarding the use of drones for search and rescue, Reynolds said. "And so that's something that we're actively involved in—not only the training but also helping law-enforcement agencies in the various states work with their state legislators to set up rules, regulations and laws that help maintain the sanctity of privacy while also giving law-enforcement some latitude to use this equipment. We're all aware of issues of privacy because we don't want our privacy invaded either." Other assistance includes helping law-enforcement agencies to obtain a certificate of authorization from the FAA allowing them to fly above 400 feet for searches and other specific emergency circumstances.

"So part of our challenge is selling our mission with this new technology," Reynolds said. "And we're being proactive. And that's a very good word. We're being proactive to build-in all of the possible safeguards that we can to ensure that the technology is utilized for the purpose intended and in a legal manner. Our mission is one thing: search and rescue, *bringing loved ones home.*"

THIRTEEN

On Leadership

*"In times of war or uncertainty there is a special
breed of warrior ready to serve our Nation's call.
A common man with uncommon desire to succeed."*

*—excerpt from the Navy SEAL Creed,
read by Capt. Ronald Yeaw, US Navy SEAL,
retired, Aug. 29, 2018*

C apt. Ronald Yeaw knows a thing or two about leadership. During his 30-year military career, which includes having commanded Naval Special Warfare Development Group, a.k.a. SEAL Team Six, from 1990 until 1992, he's seen it all—from the die-hard commitment shared by all who lead, follow and soldier on in military service to the ultimate sacrifice that all of them are expected to offer and many are destined to make.

For his own service, Yeaw has been awarded forty-five medals and decorations, including the Superior Service Medal, four Bronze Star medals and the Purple Heart.

On Aug. 29, 2018, as an official PLI ambassador and the first recipient of the organization's CEO Select Honoree distinction, Yeaw addressed attendees of the 2018 Project Lifesaver International Annual Conference, held in Orlando, Florida. The audience encompassed PLI staff and board, as well as member agents from numerous police and sheriffs' departments, and other public-safety organizations from throughout North America. The distinguished speaker drew parallels between the military, law enforcement and PLI, highlighting their alignment in terms of dedication, purpose, honor and integrity in pursuit of the mutual cause to protect others.

Yeaw congratulated Saunders on approaching twenty years serving countless most-vulnerable members of society, in line with the Navy SEAL team code's "steadfast resolve to never give up, never give in, and never leave a man behind." It's a section of the code that Yeaw takes especially to heart, not only as a steward of the ethos but also as a recipient of its manifestation. He referenced multiple examples of fellow SEALs' extreme integrity along that line, including his own experience when, in 1968, as a member of the first US Navy SEAL team ever to be deployed into combat, he was critically injured in Vietnam by a grenade. Debris riddled the entire left side of his body, disabling him, Yeaw recalled. And *his* chief refused to leave him behind.

"One of the reasons I'm so endeared with Project Lifesaver International is that your motto, 'Bringing Loved Ones Home,' closely parallels the SEAL motto of never leaving a man behind," he stated to the crowd. "Project Lifesaver International is the embodiment of that calling" to protect the weak, the sick and the vulnerable, and leave no one behind.

"I am alive today because on March 13, 1968, no one left me behind," Yeaw asserted. "And thanks to Project Lifesaver International, the same can be said for over 3,400 individuals living with cognitive impairments who have been rescued by your organization. Like the Navy SEALs, Project Lifesaver International will never stop bringing our loved ones home."

THE TRAITS THAT COUNT

In his book "When Leadership Mattered: Inspiring stories of twelve people who changed the world," author Baxter Ennis featured anecdotes highlighting life-changing—and ultimately world-changing—"moments of destiny" in the lives of fellow mere humans who accomplished notably great and widely impactful feats in their lifetimes. Many, like Saunders, had military backgrounds or political authority, or both. Many had become known for their remarkable visionary powers and their willingness and abilities to realize them, and many for their protective and empowering advocacy for people most vulnerable to the societal norms of their eras. Others were hailed for their brilliant business ideas, inspiring management or otherwise influential styles. Despite the differences in their stations and circumstances, key common threads bind their legacies, most dominantly:

1. All operated from compelling beliefs and principles which they held dear and were driven, with purpose and intention, to honor.

2. All had been groomed and "prepared" in life by what they made of their individual pursuits, opportunities and experiences.

3. Each recognized the junctures where their drive and competence were exactly what was needed in some critical effort, and they assumed the right or responsibility to act when opportunity presented.

4. When push came to shove, they all embodied seemingly tireless perseverance and tenacity—especially in the face of adversity.

Abraham Lincoln, Martin Luther King Jr., Susan B. Anthony, Patrick Henry, Theodore Roosevelt, William Wilberforce, even Steve Jobs and the others—all faced resistance, all faced adversity, all fought internal and/or external beasts of their own. What marked the difference-makers? They made the decision to face their beasts. They all refused to be slain by circumstance for as long as they could fight—even if it meant, as it did for some, that they *would* die from the fight. They seemed to understand the battle between apathy and passion, the contradiction between inertia and mobilization, the inevitable influences of passivity vs. boldness and decisiveness—and they chose sides. Each of Ennis' select subjects stood resolute in their sense of purpose, mission and integrity and remained focused on the big picture and the objectives that supported it.

The same can be said for some of Saunders' own personal role models, including US Army Gen. George Patton, President Ronald Reagan, and retired US Army Lt. Gen. Harold "Hal" Moore Jr.

Moore, who died at age ninety-four in February 2017, had been one of the most esteemed and admired combat leaders in recent US history and was the co-author and subject of several books, including "We Were Soldiers Once . . . and Young," one of Saunders' favorites by far.

Throughout his own extensive career, Saunders routinely taught classes in leadership to fellow members of military and civil service sectors, including the Civil Air Patrol and the Virginia Defense Force. He derived examples, ideology and his own insightful perspectives from his lifelong study of the subject and of those who modeled it well. So it should be no surprise that, when asked what leadership qualities they found most prominent, impressive and effective in Saunders, those who know him best said this:

- Highly motivated and passionate.
- Purposeful.
- Protective.
- Visionary.
- Goal-oriented.
- Structured and regimented.
- Hands-on.
- Dedicated; unwavering commitment.
- Articulate, motivational, inspiring.
- Integrity.
- Strong work ethic.
- Understanding and supportive.
- Bullheaded.
- Calm and logical in crisis.
- Driven.
- Confident.
- Adventuresome.
- Tenacious.
- Persistent.
- Courageous.
- Caring.
- Kind.
- Funny.
- Compassionate.

One early morning in 2017, Saunders relaxed into his thick-backed office chair and pondered the subject himself. References pertaining to his days commanding SWAT, his military training, poignant quotes and mottos, teaching, and stories about the lives and feats of combat leaders—all stepped up on cue as he set the stage for the next hour. When asked his take on whether leaders are born or bred, Saunders seemed to lean toward *born* and pointed to books that featured generals Patton and Moore.

"You know what I see in both of these men?" he asked. "They both have similar qualities: they care about their people. They care about the mission. They care about the organization. And they care about the success of the mission and doing what it takes to accomplish that *with your people in mind*."

What else makes a good leader? "That's an age-old question," Saunders said. He did his best to answer, based upon what he's read, witnessed, learned, taught and experienced, and on the never-ending assessment of his own successes and failures.

"The things that make a good leader are intangible," he said. They're the stuff of talent, nature, mindset, action and resolve. High rankers include the ability to inspire and communicate; the willingness to be out front and not in the rear; the willingness to take calculated chances, despite the risk of failure; the ability to turn a failure into a success or a lesson; and a dogged sense of faith, confidence and tenacity regardless of circumstances.

And intentions matter. They're a compass by which directions are chosen and courses get mapped and navigated. Whoever first proclaimed that the road to hell is paved with good intentions may or may not be correct. But it's sure as hell that every highway to honor *is*.

PURPOSE, PASSION AND MISSION

Saunders' unquestionable sense of purpose, and the passion and drive with which he channels it, prompted both Yeaw and Carter, independent of each other, to define him as a "superb leader."

"He's very personally devoted to his organization," Yeaw attested. "He created the organization to serve a purpose," and he's doing everything in his power to ensure that it does, he explained. As any good military leader would approach a mission on the battlefield, Saunders is simply hell-bent on fulfilling the organization's objectives and goals.

Their assessments reflect Saunders' own results-oriented mindset. "One of the biggest things a leader's got to have is a *passion* to *lead* and *succeed* in a task. And he has to have a passion for that task," he opined. "Because, let's face it: If you really care about something, you're really gonna put everything into it."

Saunders can't recall his sense of mission ever being absent. "I think I've had it all my life," he said. "Like when I was in school, I founded a fraternity. Why? Because I felt like there was a need for it. And some of the other fraternities were being so picky about who they let in. So I figured, *we'll just create our own damn fraternity, then!*" He laughed.

"I think I've always had this idea that if something needs to be done, and you can't find anybody to do it, or if what's out there already is not satisfactory, then it's incumbent upon you to do it. And I think it goes back to that saying that Jack Jacobs adopted: 'If not now, when? If not you, who?'"

Jacobs, a retired decorated US Army colonel and Medal of Honor recipient, co-authored *If Not Now, When?: Duty and Sacrifice in America's Time of Need*, another one of Saunders' go-to books for inspiration on living a life of courage, mission and integrity.

"Now I didn't know that saying back then," Saunders continued, "but I think it applies. And not only to me, but to anybody. You know, if you're not going to do it *now*, when is it going to happen? And if *you're* not going to do it, who's going to do it?

"I've always had that sense," he said. "And I like to create things, I guess. Like the narcotics squad in the police department: I felt like there was a need for it, and nobody was listening, nobody was doing anything, so I started doing it on my own, off-duty. Eventually, they saw a need for it," adopted the sense of purpose and mission and got on board.

"So I think a leader is also somebody who has a vision," Saunders concluded, "and who can get like-minded people around them, and can bring them into a group with a common purpose and goal and engage and empower them to complete that mission."

VISION

Saunders' influence and reputation as a man who has dedicated his life to public safety are well-known and present throughout southeastern Virginia, Carter noted, "but it does not stop there." What's more impactful and impressive is that the concept of resting on one's laurels seems to completely elude Saunders, leaving a clear path for momentum and all the energy it carries to manifest a logical continuum—an effort that's bound to thrive indefinitely not by virtue of his everlasting involvement but by virtue of a *vision empowered.*

"One person had a vision to help others and save lives," Carter said of Saunders. "He brought it to life, grew it from a localized idea to a multi-state idea, and then expanded it to an international program." That's impactful. That's impressive. That's a vision of a lifetime.

Reynolds calls it "incredible" when he trains PLI agents. "I tell them this is a program started by a cop sitting around at his desk, thinking, *we gotta do something better,*" he said. He uses Saunders' story to instill in young police officers and firefighters that if they have an idea, if they see a vision of how and why to solve a problem, they should pursue it. No matter how far-fetched it may seem, "with tenacity and backbone and follow-through, it could come to fruition."

No doubt, Saunders' visionary prowess was enhanced by practice, opportunity and affirmation during his law-enforcement career, when vision had as much to do with recognizing a potential threat as it did with envisioning the appropriate counteractions.

At the very least, Saunders knew inherently that "you need to be ahead of things, not behind them," he said. "And the one thing that I always had a problem with law enforcement was that we were always reactive instead of being proactive. Instead of thinking *Whoa, wait a minute, we got a problem coming, we need to start dealing with this, we need to be thinking about this,* many agencies did not do that."

But willful ignorance only works for a short time, Saunders said. Before you know it, the problem has carved a trail of destruction, and now you have to chase its wily ass. So the bottom line is this: "Do you want to be on top of it, or do you want to be dragging behind, trying to catch up?"

Foresight is a gift to be acknowledged and valued. It's the very first vision—even if dark, ugly and somewhat indiscernible—of something requiring illumination, demanding a closer look; something that, if overlooked, hindsight may one day claim for its own record of tragic errors and ironic jokes.

True visionaries know foresight intimately, and they trust it like a twin. And only into such an internal environment of respect and preparedness for it will the gift of responsive vision enter, complete with blueprints for its success to be interpreted and implemented by a willing and proactive recipient.

Saunders has the talent to think outside the box regarding improvements, expansion and implementation, Carter said. And when he looks at new ideas, he looks deeper than what's presented; "he looks inside of the new ideas to see if they are good and will work."

PLI's Canadian acolyte Police Chief Rick Derus concurs. He believes that one of Saunders' greatest accomplishments has been forcing change at Project Lifesaver to ensure that the latest and most effective technology is available to chapter agencies at a reasonable cost. "As one can imagine," Derus said, "technology changes at a rapid pace." And it takes a person with futuristic vision to keep an eye fixed on that horizon and be ready to pounce as new potential emerges. The upgrading and evolution of equipment at PLI over the years has resulted in better, more reliable offerings at lower prices. "If Chief Saunders did not drive this, the long-term viability of Project Lifesaver would be in doubt," he said. "As chairman of the Board of Trustees, I'm grateful that he has accomplished so much" on the technology front.

EGO

Bringing a vision forth takes confidence. But taking it as far as you can will likely require a bullheaded—if not absolutely unreasonable—belief in your own abilities.

Let's just call it what it is . . .

"You gotta have some ego," Saunders said.

Call it ego, pride, extreme self-confidence or whatever fuels your plane, but if honorable intentions and behavior stay in the lead, there's nothing wrong with a souped-up inner drive and having something to prove—to yourself and to the world—when attempting to create enhancements to the forces of good.

Imagine a world devoid of anything initiated from or heightened by ego: No stunning film, stage or musical performances; no memoirs or self-help books born of the legacies and successes of others; no 'world's greatest gourmet cupcakes;' no personal computers atop our desks or in our pockets; and no architecture so divine and inspiring that it draws people from around the world to stroll silently through, gaze in reverence and drop their jaws in awe.

But egos require fuel. The best type for Saunders' engine is a balanced mix of internal gratification and external reward.

"I always liked being part of a special unit, one where the challenges were a little bit more than status quo, one that *did* a little bit more than status quo," Saunders said. It's a deeper level of commitment, "a step above." He's heard it said that Special Forces and SEAL teams all share this trait. And working with them, "I had become part of something that is not the norm but is set apart because of the things it does and the accomplishments that result and what it took to get there," he explained.

Incidentally, Saunders had recently returned from a trip to where California Congresswoman Maxine Waters, a politically active supporter of Alzheimer's awareness and patient protection, had presented him with The People of Distinction Humanitarian Award in the 'Unsung Hero' category. "It felt good that Project Lifesaver was getting some recognition, especially on that level," he said of the distinction, "and it was nice that we were included in a number of other people who were doing some tremendous work."

Badges, patches, and other displays of belonging, achievement and recognition have always incentivized him. For example, "the Special Forces wear a green beret, the SEALs wear a Trident, and we wore a SWAT tab," he said. "It sets you somewhat apart. It shows that you took the extra step, that you were willing to put more out there than the average person. You know, you're willing to go beyond that. Sure, you get the internal gratification, but it also lets the world know, 'I did this. I'm part of this organization. And I had to work hard, I had to do extra things, I had to get down and dirty,' or whatever it was, but that made you part of that."

On another note—although he hates the word—"you've gotta have some *politician* in you," Saunders said. "I guess I've learned more about that since I've been in Project Lifesaver than when I had a command level in the police department, but I've never been a good politician. Because I'm going to tell you what it *is*; I'm not going to tell you what I think you should hear or what you want to hear."

Some have accused him of being too direct, but directness shouldn't be confused with arrogance, callousness or overinflated ego. Those are independent traits that can, but don't always, coexist.

"You know, when I started doing this, I was a cop," he said. "I had a cop mentality; I had a military mentality. So I always had the 'Damn the torpedoes, full speed ahead!' attitude. And I think it helped in a lot of ways, and I think sometimes it didn't."

Saunders simply comes from an alternative perspective: Withholding the truth based upon the assumption that others can't handle it wastes precious time and can put everyone in a bad position due to lack of information. While he doesn't desire to be confrontational, he does want people to know where he's coming from, what he's thinking, what he's doing and why. "That way, there's no misunderstanding" and no time wasted, he said.

So is that ego? Or is it in fact a respect for the others involved, and a show of confidence in their good judgement and their ability to act accordingly?

"I'm sure there were times when I probably could have been a little more discerning in how I said something, but I wasn't," he admitted. "So I look back and try to learn from that. But I don't like it when somebody is all politician and no action," he said. "I think you have to hit a happy balance. And I've started to try to balance that a little better. . . . But still, I'm going to tell you directly where I'm coming from."

He unloaded a few examples of his ongoing tightrope tread.

In the past, "when I'd really go into temper or rage was mainly when I was dealing with the SWAT team," he recalled. "It was when we were in training and I didn't feel like they were giving what they needed to give. They weren't giving the full effort.

"One night we were training. And we were running through the different drills and movements, and it was like we were always doing . . . sure enough, something would happen because of lack of concentration. Somebody would mess up. Not because they didn't know what to do, but because they weren't thinking. And finally I got to the point when I said, 'Listen. Right now, if they called the SWAT team out, I'd refuse to go. Because you guys do not have your shit together. You're gonna get somebody hurt, you're gonna get somebody killed. And I'm gonna tell you right now'—and of course, I was really fired up—'that until you guys can get your act together, I don't want anything to do with you.' And I turned around, got in my car and drove off.

"Well, I got a phone call the next morning," he continued. "They'd had a heart-to-heart. And I think that sometimes, that's the kind of thing you have to do. You've got to get their attention. After all, just like one of the phrases that I always told them after every mission we did: You're only as good as the last operation. You're only as good as the last thing you did. You cannot sit on your laurels, it doesn't work. You've got to constantly keep improving; you've got to keep moving ahead; you've got to be thinking ahead. You've got to do it right, and do it right every time. And if you make a mistake, make your mistake, own up to it, correct it and move on."

Saunders stays mindful that his people have egos, and he respects the precarious balancing act required to help keep them intact. Gratitude and dignity go a long way toward ego health and preservation.

"I feel like every time we do something well, I need to thank the people who were involved. Because they put it out there," Saunders said. "They put it out there hard, and they don't have to choose to do that. So I think I need to show them that I am grateful for what they've done and how they did it and what the result was."

By the same token, "If you're going to chew anybody out, do it in private and do it in a way that they're going to remember it," he urges. "I'm not saying get out there and holler and scream, because the best chewing out I ever got was from a captain who chewed me out one time, when I was a sergeant.

"This other guy and I were on the radio," he recalled, "and we got a little more playful with the transmission than we should have. So we got a call from the captain to meet him in his office. We walked in there, and he's sitting there, and he looked at me, and he looked at the other sergeant, and he said, 'A lot of people listen to that radio traffic.' And he was very calm. 'Do you feel that you were as professional as you should have been on that radio a few minutes ago?' And we were stunned. I mean, he could not have hit us between the eyes any better. He didn't raise his voice, he didn't scream, he didn't holler. And then he said, 'I trust you'll think about that. Dismissed.'

"Beautiful," Saunders said, laughing. "The most beautiful ass-chewing I ever got. He made his point, he got it across, and he made us feel like, *Man, that was so stupid.*

"I think some of the best chewing-outs come with very few words and very little emotion. I think you need to hit that point; you need to hit *where is the problem*, and make them realize what they've done and how dumb it was.

"I try to think about that," Saunders said. "I never try to destroy a person. Instead I go back to that chewing out I got and the impact it had on me."

He's heard it said, and he subscribes, that a manager manipulates people but a leader gets out in front and leads them. And he believes that good leaders move around through different styles as necessary.

"Some people call it situational leadership," Saunders said. "I just think that you try to develop the ability to do what you have to do to get people to accomplish the task at hand. Now, is that a *motivating*, or is it a little bit of an *ass-chewing*? Is it *thanking* them?" It depends upon the individuals and the situation, he said. And at some points a leader has to make changes to get something done. "You have to recognize that, too."

Integrity demands that the ego be balanced, or leveraged, by a consistent pursuit of and alignment with best intentions. That process requires reflection and introspection, and overall adherence begets internal gratification.

"I think if you don't reflect on the things you did, or why you did them, and whether they were right or wrong or could you have done something differently, you're headed for certain failure," Saunders said. "There's always a different way to do something, and if you make a mistake, you need to admit it to yourself and say, 'OK, how could I have done that a little better? How could I have gotten a little more motivation there? If I wanted to accomplish this, how could I have done it better or differently than what I did?'"

Saunders' bottom line is this: A good leader must be confident and insistent enough of certain things, "and that's going to take somebody who's got some ego. But it's going to have to be a *balanced* ego," he cautioned. "Listen to the other side of a story. Know when to step out," he advises. "And these can be hard lessons," he said. "That's not something that somebody can teach you sometimes. It's something that you have to learn through getting your eyes blackened and your nose bloodied and your feelings hurt. You need to know when to step out and say, 'Damn the torpedoes, full speed ahead,' and you also need to know when to kind of fall back and change your course a little bit."

Saunders knows that he could have applied his talents, strengths and virtues to any number of alternative career paths. He'd had the musical chops in his youth and young adulthood to turn pro as a drummer, guitarist or bass guitarist. He could have pursued teaching, entrepreneurship, public speaking or countless other avenues. But in the end, his ego's internal gratification pump runs on *ultimate impact*. He's driven by conquest for the benefit of others.

"The most satisfaction I have ever gotten in anything was when I was able to be part of something that was successful and that left me with a good feeling that we helped people," Saunders said. "When I did something that made a difference to somebody, or made somebody feel good, or helped somebody, it made me feel good. And I like that feeling. So why not just keep doing it?"

The answer to that question depends on the ego's alignment with best intentions and one's confidence and willingness to continue stepping up to the personal call to duty.

PERSONAL RESPONSIBILITY, ATTITUDE, FORTITUDE

Any seasoned people-watcher can address the contrast in human behavior: some people sit back, stand off and distance themselves from a situation to avoid risk—the risk of becoming accountable for the outcome. People like Saunders see the same situation and don't understand why others retreat or refuse to even acknowledge it. What gives?

"I've encountered guys who have had no desire to be out front at all—*none*," Saunders said. "And they'll tell you, 'No, I don't wanna do it. You tell me what you want; I don't want to lead.'"

Saunders understands. "Many times I've been a follower," he said. "I have no problem following. If you've got somebody out there who's doing a great job, and everything's going great, I have no problem following." He didn't lead when he trained with the SEALs, and he followed a lot while in the service. "I was one of the grunts," he said, laughing. "And I stepped in and did whatever they told me to do. And if they asked me for an opinion, I gave it to them. If they asked me for help, I gave it to them. Until I got to a position where, *OK, now I get to lead . . . what do I do now?*" he joked.

But in fact, Saunders noted, "you can't lead unless you can follow.

"Now, a leader may delegate authority to complete a task," he continued, and the ability to do so is often mission-essential. "But one of the things that leadership does bring with it is responsibility. Ultimately the leader is responsible for the outcome and must accept that. Like the captain of a ship: I don't care what happens on that ship; it's his or her responsibility. I just think that's something you either want to do or you don't want to do," he said. "And if you want to do it, then you accept that risk comes with it."

On another note, "when you look at people who just don't want to act, I think that they're afraid to fail," Saunders said. They don't take responsibility because they don't want to be the ones responsible for undesirable conclusions. But the logic is porous, he posed. "How are you going to get it done if nobody's going to step up?

"A good leader will stand up," Saunders said. "They will *seek* responsibility, and they will *take* responsibility for their actions. And I think that is one of the things that we need to see more of."

Some scary things—parachuting, for instance—only put the risk-taker at risk. But fear of failure carries a lot more weight for those who also assume responsibility for the lives of others. It's an uncommon breed of leader who answers that call. And yes, *somebody* has to answer it.

Saunders set his hands on a short stack of books written by and about military leaders. He referenced the movie "We Were Soldiers" and mentioned that guys like Hal Moore always remained top of mind as he taught leadership to others. "Hal Moore," he said, prior to making a case for his affinity. "They were in a tremendous battle with the North Vietnamese army. And all of a sudden his superiors gave him an order via radio and said, 'We want you out of there; we want you back here to brief us.' His response told me what kind of leader he was. He said, 'I will not leave my people in the middle of a fight. That is a ridiculous order, and I will not follow it.'

"He had always told his people, 'When we go into a battle, I will be the first in and the last out,'" Saunders continued. "And he always said, 'We will leave no one behind.'

"That kind of stuff means something to people. I mean, if I was sitting there as a soldier, and I heard that, I'd follow this guy through the gates of hell. Because I'd know he cared."

Saunders thought back on his police years. "Every time we went out on a SWAT operation, it was scary," he recalled. "There were a lot of things that could go wrong. I think my biggest fear was that some of my people would get hurt or that somebody would get hurt because I made a mistake. So I tried to plan them carefully. You practice your craft. You train. And that's why a lot of the military training that I could get, I took it. I figured the more I know, the more situations that I have been in, the more I can handle myself in any situation, the better off I'm going to be in leading this team."

His mission with Project Lifesaver is more than an assignment, more than a full-time job; it's a 24/7 lifestyle. Before and after hours, unless he's focused on something else, he's mentally wrapped up in PLI. Even sleep won't guarantee respite.

Formatively speaking, Saunders believes that people develop not only from positive influences but also through negative experiences. Whatever the loss, the key to ultimately gaining from a negative experience lies in reevaluating it, adjusting to it, and reframing it as an opportunity to learn and improve. Never let fear of failure stunt your growth. Never let it rule your life. "Negative things are going to happen," he assured. "You can be the most well-intended person in the world, but things are going to happen; Murphy's Law is going to get in there. Things are going to go wrong; things are going to go bad; you're going to make mistakes." The only way to avoid making mistakes is to avoid doing anything at all, he reasoned, "and *that's* a mistake."

And so is wallowing in the wake of a bad experience, Saunders noted. "When something happens, like we have a problem or something, I internalize that. That really works on me, upsets me," he said. "But you have to develop an inner sense of acceptance and moving on." Acknowledge the experience, feel the pain or the regret or the emotions, "but you've got to push through it. Learn from it." Do a personal after-action report, but don't overanalyze, whine or feel sorry for yourself. And don't let it destabilize your sense of confidence. Recheck your intentions, balance analysis with acceptance, reset your ego if necessary, and move on.

"I constantly want to find new and better ways to handle things," Saunders said, "and I'm always telling the staff and others that we have to drive forward constantly." Even with success, he said, "we can never rest on our laurels. We can never say, 'Well, we've done it great to this point.' It's like I used to tell the SWAT team: You're only as good as your last operation. What about the next one? You think for one minute that people are going to remember all the great things that you all did if you screw up one time really bad? *No*." This is life or death. "One 'Aww, shit' will erase a thousand 'Atta boys.'

"I struggle every day with these things, trying to think of how to do this, and how to do it right," Saunders said. "Am I right all the time? No. I don't think anybody is. And anyone who tells you they don't think about this, or they don't second-guess themselves, they're lying." You can be a great leader, he said, "but you're still going to second-guess yourself in areas. You may not do it in the heat of the moment; you may not do it today, but somewhere down the road you'll wonder, *Could I have done that differently; could I have made a better decision?*" That's the nature of responsibility.

According to Saunders, it doesn't help that the virtue of personal responsibility has been watered down by the showering of delusions of entitlement. And "that does not say much for society as a whole," he said.

"I don't believe anybody's *entitled* to anything," Saunders asserted; "All that tells me is that you don't think you're responsible for anything you do." He wouldn't tolerate that attitude in himself, and he won't have it in his organization. The entitlement mindset is so counter to that of leadership, so counterproductive to any worthy mission.

Perhaps a person of entitlement mindset can "lead," according to some definition of the word; perhaps he or she can "lead" as the strongest entitled person at the forefront of a pack of them, "but when it all comes down to what a true leader needs to do, I think that's where they're going to fall short," Saunders said. "Why? Because they think they're entitled to be there." Historically speaking, "no great leader ever had the idea that they were entitled to be a leader. They had a *desire* to be a leader" and a *willingness* to assume the requisite risks and responsibilities that entitled characters, by virtue of their dependent, avoidant nature, can't—and won't—handle.

The bottom line: "No pain, no gain," Saunders said. Whatever the circumstance, whatever the objective, "if you're not willing to stick your neck out there and do what you have to do to make it happen, then it's not going to happen. It's going to be the same-old same-old." We all make attempts that don't work out as expected, he concluded, "but if that is what you're going to live your life by, then you might as well just stay under that rock of inertia."

ETHICS, INTEGRITY AND INDEPENDENT THINKING

When asked for his take, Saunders' colleague Yeaw praised the "impeccable integrity in how they conduct their business" at Project Lifesaver. Saunders' high standards for best practices, and his demands that they be met if not exceeded, regardless of what other organizations accept as the status quo, serve daily to earn trust, uphold credibility and ensure iconic quality, both internally and within the market.

Where does Saunders' sense of honor and integrity originate? "I can't remember ever *not* having it," he said. Thinking as far back as the Boy Scout years, "I can't remember ever *not* having that sense of honor or being able to trust and be trusted. And I've always thought that your reputation is the single most valuable thing you have."

The principle is as simple as it is momentous: Integrity begets trustworthiness; trustworthiness begets trust; honoring that trust begets good reputation.

"Don't go throwing that away," Saunders urges, "because when people start throwing mud at you, that reputation may be the only thing to get you through." Others will recall how you've acted with integrity and authenticity in the past, he explains, and they're inclined to stand behind you when you need them.

Scaling up the concept, the standards for ethics and integrity must be effectively conveyed and understood companywide. The culture must be one of reverence, promotion, reinforcement and representation of the organization's values. The importance of hiring people of good character cannot be overstated, because every individual's inside world directs what they contribute to the outside in terms of their personal and professional relationships and efforts.

Likewise, from every organization's inside world emanates the spirit of its people, the paradigms by which they operate, the influence they propagate, and the forces they then perpetuate whether good, bad or indifferent—and the latter two should not be options. Like the structure of a tree, from the tip of the deepest root to the tip of the highest-reaching branch, what runs through it affects its core, its growth, its health, its strength and its overall presence in the world. Consider the damage done to Project Lifesaver by two trusted employees who threw ethics and integrity out the window: the time, money and energy lost to fights that never should have happened; the growth and outreach stunted by lack of sustenance and attention; the whacking and hacking that chipped away at its protective bark of reputation.

PLI staff and volunteers understand and embrace the concept and the responsibility, Reynolds said. "Chief is very direct; he'll tell you what he thinks, and smile," he said, "and he expects honesty. We constantly talk about the importance of credibility and honesty, and Chief doesn't have to talk too much about those virtues, because he models them."

Within that context the PLI staff thrives, both as individuals who take pride in their contributions to the organization and its beneficiaries, and also in support of one another.

Disturbing trends

The erosion of ethics, integrity and independent thinking strikes Saunders as gravely destructive to American business, culture and economy. The signs of it show up in such trends as entitlement mindsets, misappropriated "heroism," inappropriate activism and intentional deceit.

"This sense of entitlement that people seem to have—that they can break the law with impunity, that they can do pretty much anything they want and there are no consequences—while that is not the norm for everybody, I think it's becoming pervasive," he said. "And I think it's becoming pervasive because the news media is making it that way. They're highlighting it, so you've got all these people out here who see it being done and think, *If they can do it, it must be OK, I can do anything I want,*" because government says it's OK "or somebody has allowed it, so it must be OK.

"I think that's a disturbing trend," Saunders said. "I think it needs to be reversed, and quickly. We've got enough threats from external sources. If we don't get a handle on how we behave, and how we act, and reinstall a sense of responsibility and morals back into this country, we're going to destroy ourselves from within. No country will have to go to war with us, just wait and pick up the pieces.

"Regarding 'heroism,' I think society has placed too much emphasis on the wrong people," Saunders added. "We banter that term around all the time, you know, 'hero, hero.' We have war heroes out there who are legitimate heroes, but because a guy catches a football and runs 90 yards and makes a touchdown, he's a 'hero.' Well, wait a minute. What about this guy over here who just saved twenty of his buddies in combat? Now *there's* a hero. Or a cop or a firefighter or a civilian who saved somebody from a burning building, or burning car, or gets in a shootout to save somebody? Guys and women who risk their lives to save other people's lives, *they're* heroes," he said. "These guys with a football, with a baseball, or with a soccer ball, they're not heroes. They're game players. They're doing what they're paid to do. They may be stars, but they're not heroes."

The same can be said for those we consider role models, especially those professional athletes, entertainers and others who seem to have made it overnight, Saunders said. First of all, not everyone who has succeeded in one area of life has necessarily earned the status of *role model.* Secondly, many who appear to have made it overnight have in fact put in thousands of hours over many years to prepare for the opportunities they were resolute enough to then embrace on the road to their success. The good fortune born of hard work, sacrifice and perseverance is natural consequence; it's authentic; it's worth more than the fortune born of luck because it requires and compounds character.

Before presuming others to be role models, "look at the kind of people they are," Saunders urges. "Look at their personal lives. Look at what they believe in, and how they act." Have they earned their place at the top of the ladder? Do they deserve to be seen as role models? Some do, and some don't, he said. "I believe that as you're climbing the rungs of the ladder, if you skip any of those rungs, through fortune or whatever, I believe you've lost something. I think you lose an appreciation of how and why you got to where you are. Sure, maybe you had some talent, and somebody saw you, and you can sing. So you go out there and you sing, and you make a ton of money, but you become a jerk."

On another note, Saunders winced at the thought of celebrity activism run amok. The attitude of actors, entertainers, athletes and other famous people espousing political philosophies from incongruous platforms strikes him as manipulative. They take the stage, field or podium, and the captive audience assumes the earful of inappropriate indoctrination. Don't fall for it, Saunders warns; the act itself is Machiavellian. "They're no different than you or I. They have their beliefs, but just because they say something doesn't make it true. I have a real problem with them espousing some of that stuff using performance contexts as a platform." What makes a celebrity an authoritative commentator on the world and all the individuals who comprise it? "I have a problem with that arrogance and misuse of influence," he said. He urges people to keep politics and cultural issues out of business and to return the focus to the quality and integrity of the products and services they provide.

As for deceit, to say that it runs rampant in the business world would be an understatement. So is it irony that the experience is so *understated*?

Newcomers often arrive naïve about the prevalence of deception until their unfortunate baptisms by fire. No one warned them. Then later, when hindsight illuminates the newly obvious, they're too busy trying to reconcile the occurrence and its consequences—or they're simply drained of energy—to coherently convey what the hell happened as a lesson for their peers. But years after his own brutal dealings, Saunders shares some reality-born wisdom for the sake of the vulnerable.

"They need to understand that there are people out there who are wolves in sheep's clothing," he said. "Don't believe or accept everything that you hear from others. Do your research. Everybody is not out there for the good of mankind.

"And be careful of people who want to come in and give you money or expand your business," he continued. "I think you need to ask some very poignant questions, like, 'Why?' and 'If it expands, what happens then?'" Saunders has learned that big companies with big checkbooks target smaller organizations for ambush. "They come in, they get that little company, and then they bring them into litigation to force them out of business so the big company can take over," he warned. The unfortunate truth is that there are people out there who are mean and ruthless, and to them, this is *just business.* "But I don't buy that crap," Saunders said. "And I think that's what's wrong with our country right now. That's one of the ills we have. People are not upfront and honest anymore. It's all about the money. It's all about 'What can I do to screw you out of what you have, so that I can have it?'. But if you're going to do business, be ethical, for Christ's sake. You know, be upfront."

Not everyone in business operates with duplicity, Saunders granted, but too many do. Critical and independent thinking go a long way toward self-preservation and protecting the vulnerable. He urges businesspeople to listen intently, think for themselves, consult with trustworthy advisors who can recognize red flags, and practice discernment. A trusting nature is sweet—sweet like blood to a shark—but can be flipped to burnt, jaded and cynical by a ruinous encounter with the wrong kind of ally.

Saunders also believes in the resurrection of a near-dead concept in business: "We've gotten away from the old 'Southern way' of doing business—a handshake, a verbal agreement, and if we have a problem we'll sit down and work it out . . . or go our separate ways," he said. "It's not that way anymore," or it's very rare, he said, "and I think it's a shame."

From the ashes of multiple betrayals and the lawsuits that set PLI back several years and more than $400,000, Saunders has plucked a few gems and forged a few new ironclad rules. One collides with everything on that topic that business and law students have heard in class lectures for ages, everything that big businesses spend big chunks of time and big bucks trying to perfect for wielding in big fights in the future: *No more written contracts in business-to-business dealings,* Saunders decided years ago.

He refuses to lock himself and his organization into a position that he couldn't exit without another resource-draining fight. If everyone's upfront, and all intentions align, contracts become irrelevant and potentially harmful as a hindrance to human judgement and organizational progress. According to Saunders, "If I can't look you in the eye and trust you, then you and I don't need to be doing business."

Some of the companies that pressured him into signing contracts ended up binding him to things counter to his mission. They had told him they couldn't move ahead without a contract, but "that was bull crap," Saunders said. Legally speaking, "you can do anything you want without a contract.

"I've seen the other side, and I don't like it," he continued. "I think all it is, is greed. They always build something into those contracts so that if you find that something's wrong, and you want out, they can nail you." He sat back and shrugged. "Let's face it: you can draw up a contract to the *nth* word, but ultimately it's all in how it's interpreted," he said. "You can look at it a million times; *you* read it, and *I* read it, and we're going to get two different meanings out of it." And the lawyers will, as well. "So what does that lead to? 'Oh, we've got to go to court and let a judge decide.'" Then how does a court or any given lawyer or even a jury interpret it?

Don't be pushed into believing that everybody in business operates with contracts; "it's just not true," Saunders warned. Too many people make contract disputes a lifestyle, a living; "they use a legal piece of paper to beat you to death," he warned. "You know, 'If you don't do what I say . . . If you don't like it, I've got a contract . . . If things go wrong, you're just gonna have to suck it up.' Well, I don't agree with that. And I'm not going to be held to that. Not anymore," he said. Contracts don't necessarily protect people, "and plenty of lawyers will tell you that on contract suits, often the only ones making any money are the lawyers. I've had enough of the money-hungry litigious trolls in today's society; I'm tired of it."

Ethically speaking, the issue again reverts to integrity. "I think that ethics have really gone out the window in a large part," Saunders said. "I believe that honor has suffered. If I can look you in the eye, and we can agree, and we can shake hands, then we're good to go. But both parties have to have that sense of honor, that we're going to make this work. Sure, we could run into bumps, but we're going to make it work, whatever we need to do, until it's exhausted to the point of mutual dissatisfaction. And even then, there's often something else you can do," he said, "but you're dealing with two parties here, and one may not believe it. So you want to have that flexibility, and that honor that you're going to be truthful with each other, that there's no hidden agenda going in, and that everything is upfront and aboveboard. Period. And I think that's gone by the wayside," he said. "I think the companies we dealt with years ago had hidden agendas, and after they got us into signing the contract, that's when their agendas became visible. Then they started with 'Oh, we got you now!' OK, but from now on, if I don't sign a contract, you haven't *got me*, have you?"

Saunders has no problem with writing a memorandum of understanding or agreement, thus putting on paper who intends to do what, he said, "but it's not going to be a contract, and I am not going to treat it as a contract. Instead, we're going to talk in plain English. I don't need 'wherefore' and 'therefore' and 'therein' language," he mused. Just outline it in simple terms: "What is it that we want to do, how do we want to do it, and that's what we're going to do. That way, if we can't do it, and we can't agree, we go our separate ways. Done. We're both free to walk away," he said. No lawsuits, no one party forcing the other to comply with anything that might compromise its mission, "none of that.

"Now we operate that way with all the people we deal with, and they understand," Saunders said. And it's working well, he affirmed. "We're able to talk to one another civilly; we're able to arbitrate with them if we have a disagreement. It's not like anyone's holding a hammer over the other's head. I think we're all in this for the right reasons and we understand that as you go along, things are going to change. I mean, *geez*, who do we get a blueprint from? We're making the blueprint. If we're moving along and all of a sudden we see that we need to change something for the better, we can, whereas sometimes you get into a contract situation and you can't do it. So what do you do? You stagnate," he said. "But I'm not going to operate like that. Things are too fluid. Like I said, we are the ones making the blueprint as we go. This way we can go to a supplier and say, 'OK, here's what we're finding, we need to do this.' And we're able to sit down and work it out with them."

It's simple. It's natural law vs. courtroom law: "If you can't do business with me on a handshake, and look me in the eye, and if we can't operate from common sense, then don't do business with me," Saunders states firmly. "That's just the way it is."

He'd like to see new generations of businesspeople thinking and acting along this line, outside the box of so-called conventional wisdom being fed to them from elsewhere. "I think that's one of the problems we see today in some of the education," he noted. "They bypass common sense." He doesn't even subscribe to the notion that everyone needs or should pursue a college degree. "They're teaching all of this abstract theory, which doesn't mean a damn thing in real life. That's my opinion," he said, "for whatever it's worth."

TENACITY AND PERSEVERANCE

"Never let anyone destroy your vision. . . .
Complete the mission. . . .
When there's a will, there's a way."
But remember this: "The only easy day was yesterday."

"Bullheaded?" Saunders again considered the charge. "Yeah," he said. "And I think my wife would agree."

But it's just the face of the spirit of commitment. "If you're not committed to something, you're going to quit as soon as it gets tough or the going gets hard," Saunders said. "So when I'm committed, unless you can really convince me that it's a bad idea, then I'm going, somehow, to move on it."

Much of Saunders' commitment he owes to what he has initiated as a visionary.

"You're seeing that things aren't working, and you're thinking, *How about if we try it this way?"* he explained. He thought back on decades' worth of trials, errors, setbacks and strides on the police and search-and-rescue fronts. Had he not had a passion for problem-solving, had he not yielded to his visions and drafted them for others to see, and had he not had the confidence to present his ideas and the gumption to stand by them, what would any of those epiphanies, visions and revelations ever mattered? He believed they mattered, and he committed himself to that belief.

But that spark is only the start.

"Just because you think it's a good idea, do you think it's going to happen overnight?" Saunders posed. "It's probably not," he assured. "Do you think that if you go to somebody and say, 'I think this is a great idea, let's do it,' that person will jump on board?" That's not likely either, he forewarned; "you're always going to hit resistance."

Those who know Saunders best attribute his success to what some would consider an almost superhuman tenacity and perseverance. Without it, one doesn't have a shot when up against resistance and adversity. But it's still no guarantee.

"One thing I've learned is to pick your battles," Saunders said. "Did I lose some? Sure, I lost some. But what you try to do is pick the right time and place. Pick your battles. Have your strategy. Have in mind what you want to do, how you want to do it, and pick the moment you want to put it to them."

And then be prepared for the likelihood that fewer people than you'd expected will actually *get it*.

"What really is tough is when you put it out there and people look at you like you have two heads," he continued. "Like, 'What are you, out of your mind?' And, 'Oh, no, you don't want to carry that to the chief; oh, boy, he'll really be pissed!'" Despite the possible responses, you have to put it out there, Saunders said, "so you reason, *What's he gonna do? He can't eat me!*"

Don't take the naysayers personally, Saunders advises. Some resist simply because they lack the gift of being visionary. "With others, it could be personality resistance; it could be that *We've done this for 20 years, and it's fine!* kind of resistance—you know, just resistance to changing, period," he said. That's where tenacity steps in. "If you want it, and you think you believe in it, just keep pushing. Keep going," he said.

Saunders referenced the ongoing push-pull for a SWAT unit at Chesapeake PD. "That was one of those 'pick your battles' situations," he recalled. "I saw how things were starting to lean, that now's the time to jump in there; don't sit back and wait, because in two weeks the chief's going to have his mind on other things. *Now* get in there! Get in there *right now*. Push it; go for it." Nobody else seemed to get it at first, "but when the deputy chief came back and said, 'Well, yeah, I really like that SWAT concept,' boy, I just jumped right back in there, full-force, both feet," he said.

"Did the push always work? Well, hell, no. No, not always," Saunders admitted, laughing. But when your inner voice is loud, clear and rational, you have to let it resound high above the din of the naysayers. Sometimes it's lonely on that frequency, but you have to stay tuned to it. That's the only way to eventually home in on an elusive target.

Perseverance

Forging inroads on the mission isn't easy on any given day. And the most trying years for Saunders were those marred by betrayal and legal fights. With saboteurs like his, who needed enemies?

But anyone rifling through the library of empowering anecdotes and quotes in Saunders' mental storehouse might suspect that those were the years he'd been preparing for all his life. From his heart to the hearts of the everyday warriors in their own good fights, let one sentiment set the cadence for all else to fall in line:

"Never let anybody destroy your vision." Take it from a guy who's camped at the front line awhile.

Not that it's easy. Some miles marched will be damn brutal; they'll beat the hell out of you if they can. But if they're beating the hell out from wherever it lives in you, let it rise, baby; let it burn. It's still yours. You possess it as much as it possesses you. Let the flames unfurl relentlessly in the face of resistance. Let the warrior that's been dormant inside you collect its power and roar and stomp its way out to your mission's defense.

"Never let anyone destroy your vision," Saunders reasserted. And take this brief from the SEALs: "The only easy day was yesterday."

Still, we're human. Shit hurts. And sucker-punches . . . well, they suck.

"When we were going through all that, there were many mornings when I just did not want to get out of bed, did not want to come in to work," Saunders recalled. "But the thing that I kept thinking was, *We started this for a particular reason. I think we're doing the right thing. I'm going to push and stay this course. I am not going to be pushed out by bullies or somebody who wants to take it away from us.*

"One thing I've found is that you go through every emotion in the book," he continued. "And you can do it all in five minutes every time something happens. You deal with anger, anxiety, fear . . . The fear is, *what happens if I lose?* And then doubt: *Should I just hang it up? Should I just say OK, that's it?*

"Hell, no," he said, recalling that he'd had to conjure up his fire: "To hell with those people! Who do they think they are? They think they're big shots, and they're just gonna run all over us, they're gonna drive us into the ground and get rid of us? That's not going to happen. Never quit. There's always one more thing you can do," he reminded himself. "If I'm going down, I'm going down kicking and screaming, and they're gonna know they've been in a hell of a fight. You know, they're gonna bleed, so to speak, as much as I do.

"And we kept looking for 'one more thing you can do,'" Saunders recalled. "In the litigation, I kept looking: *What's one more thing we can do to win this? What's one more thing?* And the lawyers and I talked daily. I just was not going to succumb to the adversaries. I felt like we were in it for the right reasons, and they weren't. And I was not going to let them prevail."

The same mindset also saw Saunders through challenges in the realms of technology, marketplace competition, finances and more, according to Derus. Yet through the years, no matter what forces may descend, "Gene will passionately defend and promote Project Lifesaver," he said. "And it is notable that even during the challenging economic times," he added, "Project Lifesaver has continued to grow, expand and find funding in a very difficult economic climate."

In terms of greatest challenges in business, funding takes the prize. When asked how he feels about entrepreneurs presenting to venture capitalists and other investors, especially on TV, Saunders took a cautious tone.

"I don't like the idea that these people have to get up in front of an audience, and these omnipotent people out here with all this money are going to judge them," he said. "Because I was judged, and I was told that Project Lifesaver was the craziest idea that people had ever heard. If I'd had to stand up there in front of those investors, what do you think they would have told me?" he hypothesized. "*The same thing!*

"I don't buy into discouragement," Saunders said. "When we first started? Project Lifesaver, I had people tell me this was the craziest idea they had ever heard, it would never work, and who did I think I was, and various other sundry things," he recalled. "But we made it work. I think that if you have the passion and the desire, you can do anything. You can do whatever you want to do. But you cannot deviate," he warned. "You may have to 'massage' it as you go along, but this stuff of somebody telling you, 'That's stupid, that's a crazy idea,' that's *bull crap*," he asserted. "I don't believe in that."

In short, don't put stock in naysayers, Saunders said; they're not invested in you.

Moreover, "Sometimes I think you're dealing with lazy people who just aren't motivated to do anything, so they don't want you to do it either," he proposed. "You know, 'I didn't succeed, so I don't want you to succeed.' But how do they know what you're capable of? If I want to go bloody my head against a wall to follow my passion, what business is it of theirs? If they don't want to help, then fine, get out of my way. And if I die on the sword on the top of this hill, I did it to myself. I did it for what I believed in."

For others, the discouragement might stem from fear, Saunders said. "I firmly believe that what hampers most people in moving forward on anything is that fear that they're going to fail, that they're going to look stupid," he said. "And it's easier to quit than it is to put the effort into pushing ahead through the fear."

When people ask if he ever feared he'd fail, Saunders doesn't skip a beat. "Absolutely. Sure I did," he said. "Every time I've done something; when I was in the service, when I was in the police department. But did I sit and worry about the consequences? No." He laughed. "Did I charge ahead like a bull? Mmmmmm, probably," he guessed.

"Sometimes there may be a valid reason *not* to do something," Saunders conceded. "But does that reason override the reason to *do* it?" he poses. "You make a decision. Like with Project Lifesaver: Was there a reason *not* to do it? Well, yeah," he said, "because a lot of people thought it was crazy. And if I fail, I'm going to be playing right into their hands.

"But when I think back, I have never been one to take 'No' for a final answer," Saunders continued. "Trust your instincts. If you want to do something bad enough, you'll find a way. If you want to do it bad enough, and your passion shows, people will follow you." A leader will persevere, he urged. A leader will reason with himself or herself: "If I'm not going to do this, who's going to do it? Why shouldn't I just go ahead and do it? Like the quotes, 'If not now, when? If not *me*, who?' And the SEALs' 'Never quit.' And Hal Moore's 'When everything is failing, there's always another thing you can do; no matter what happens, there's always one more thing you can do.'

"Never quit," Saunders said, "and never take what somebody tells you as *that's the end of it*. I honestly believe all that. And good leaders prove it. I'll give you General Douglas MacArthur: they told him he couldn't go back to the Philippines. What'd he do? He went back. He pushed them and pushed them and pushed them, and they went back. They told him that in Korea, landing in Inchon was a crazy idea. The North Koreans had been pushing the Americans back, pushing everybody back. So what General MacArthur did was went around them and behind them and did an amphibious landing at Inchon. And beat the hell out of them! That is now looked at as one of the most brilliant military strategic moves ever made," Saunders said. "If China hadn't come into it, he'd have won that whole war," he noted. "But that's where he miscalculated, and that's another story." He swiveled his chair and half-laughed. "But still, it's the idea that people will tell you 'You can't do it.' Thank God my wife never told me that," he said. Still today, "sometimes I'll come up with stuff, and I tell Tommy [Carter], and he'll look at me like I have three heads," he admitted. "But he goes with it." And sometimes it turns out that three heads are better than one.

Carter said he's impressed and inspired by Saunders' "strong constitution and dedication" to see Project Lifesaver thrive. "It's his baby," he said. "It's his child. And he's protective of it. He wants it to survive and grow up. And it is."

On another note, "I'm not saying that I'll never reach a point when it's time for me to quit," Saunders said. And sometimes a leader has to regroup or redirect, he advised; but don't let the naysayers get under your skin. He leaned forward and stared intently. "I believe," he said, "I honestly believe, that some people just don't have the guts to go after their dream. And they're looking for something to tell them that they can't do it, something to use as a crutch," so they can avoid even trying, he said. "But look at all these people out there who *have* achieved their dreams, and people told them the same thing: 'You can't do that; that won't work; that's the stupidest thing I've ever heard.'" Don't let it in, he urges. "Sure, you may bloody your head a couple of times," he said. "You very well may. But wipe the blood off and keep going. And if you can't go over the hill, go around it. There's always a way." The pioneers tunneled through all the odds, but "where would this country be if everybody just decided, 'Oh, well, somebody said I couldn't do it, so that's it!'"

Saunders had always hoped he'd had the forces of good on his side. "But you know, good doesn't always win out over evil," he conceded. "So every day, you get up with the idea that *I am not going to let them beat me today.* And you take it one day at a time. But even though you're taking it a day at a time, you need to be thinking: *There's always something you can do. There's always something more you can do.*

"And when something goes wrong, there is always another way to do it. If the first way fails, there is another way. And there's another way. And there's another. Even when things look like they're at the very end, there's always something you can do. There's always a way to do it. You just have to find it. Keep reaching. Keep looking. Keep driving forward," he said. "At my own lowest points, did I ever think about quitting? Oh, yeah," he admitted. "But I couldn't. I just couldn't. Because once you give up, that's it. You've given up. I think your whole thought process shuts down, your motivation shuts down, you just reach a point where you don't have it in you anymore to fight," he warned. "And I was not going to be defeated. I was not going to go down, or have this organization go down that way.

"And so I would tell anybody, 'Never give up. Never quit.' When things are going to shit, step back and say, 'There's another way to do this. I just gotta find it.' You might fall back and regroup, but you don't quit the mission," he said. "Where there's a will, there's a way. You can find it, you just have to keep pushing. Complete the mission and go for the gold."

*"He is literally the Henry Ford of Project Lifesaver.
I have witnessed his vision being repeated over and
over again as new chapters come on board."*

—*Rick Derus, deputy chief of the Windsor
Police Service, Ontario, Canada; chairman of the
Board of Trustees, Project Lifesaver International*

Communication

It's not only by his vision and the tenacity with which he manifests it that Gene Saunders conquers the seemingly unsurmountable, Derus and others have noted. It's also by the way that Saunders *communicates* the vision and its significance—the way he gets his point across; how he illuminates his own very clear vision and the relevance of its impact for others to behold. He knows the power of good teams, he understands the critical role of persuasive communication in the effort to inspire and mobilize those teams, and he projects his confidence onto those who strive to receive and reflect it.

"I have heard entire rooms go silent as Gene speaks of his first-hand experiences while conducting Project Lifesaver rescues," Derus attested. Simultaneously, Saunders encourages audiences and others to embrace his vision as their own, from a kindred sense of purpose, passion and duty, as champions for the cause and allies in the mission.

"I'm very impressed with the manner in which he does it," Derus said of the tireless advocacy. "Gene comes across as an expert in the field, but he does it in a manner that doesn't belittle others," he explained. "He simply wants to educate anyone who will listen about how valuable this program is. He is literally the Henry Ford of Project Lifesaver. I have witnessed his vision being repeated over and over again as new chapters come on board."

As Derus sees it, Saunders never overlooks the opportunity to promote the life-saving program and equipment. Whether he's attempting to appeal to a large group, a small-town sheriff or a member of Congress, Saunders "can always be visibly seen trying to promote Project Lifesaver," he said. "This alone is highly motivational to our members, and most certainly to the board of trustees."

But that's what it takes. "Let's face it," Saunders said: "Everything that Project Lifesaver has done has been pretty much on a grassroots level. We don't have national advertising" in big magazines or on TV, he explained. With the exception of advertising in smaller, targeted trade magazines, "it's all been word-of-mouth, grassroots, us going out and speaking" to members of the media and individuals and organizations working for a common cause. "But it's also the kind of thing you have to keep doing," he said. It's important to remain top-of-mind to members and boards, and to get in front of newcomers over time.

When asked in 2017 how many people a leader needs to get in front of in order to find an avid cheerleader, Saunders referred to Pilot International's Nancy Gray, one of his first notably integral champions. "One," he declared. "The *right* one. The right person hears it, and the next thing you know, there it goes."

Modeling

Style-wise, he's an authority but by no means an autocrat. In Saunders' ongoing mindfulness to set and uphold standards, he must count himself as much a team player as a team leader to meet his own standard of effectiveness and respectability. He's a fan of modeling that, and one bygone but indelible impression illustrates why:

Saunders and his unit had just finished basic training at Fort Knox, Kentucky. While still on station waiting for orders, they assumed duties. "One day we were out doing a police call, which is picking up trash," he recalled. "And this guy came over to us. And it was hot. Man, it was really hot. So he had on a white T-shirt and his fatigue bottoms and boots. And he asked if we would give him a hand moving a PT stand, the wooden podium from where the guy leading PT leads everybody. And they're fairly heavy. He said, 'I sure would appreciate it if you guys would give me a hand with this. I gotta move it about twenty feet.' So we thought, *OK, cool. He asked nicely; we'll go over and help him.* So we helped him move it.

"Well, when we get finished, he goes and gets his fatigue jacket and puts it on," Saunders continued. "And he's an *officer*! He could have ordered us to do it. But he didn't, and look at how we responded.

"I always felt like that's the kind of guy I want to be," Saunders said. "You know, I want to be that kind of guy who, when nobody realizes what I am, we can get things done. And when they realize whatever stature or rank or whatever I may have, they'll say, 'Now that's the kind of guy, or leader, that I want to be.'"

Some say a good leader has charisma, Saunders said. "But what is charisma?" he challenged. "A guy with charisma can lead you right into a path of destruction."

His different take: "I think a good leader has a degree of showmanship," he said. "And they know when to turn it on and when to turn it off."

He cited a scene from a movie about Gen. Patton. "He and his army were headed to relieve the 101st Airborne Division at Bastogne," Saunders began. "And they ran into all kinds of ominous weather and stiff resistance. And one of his units was trying to hold; they doubted their ability to get through alive. And Patton explodes. He went into a rage, telling them, 'We're not holding anything; we're moving forward; we're advancing, we're attacking! There are good men dying out there, and we will get there, or we will all die in the process,' or something to that effect. And he called his chaplain and said, 'I want a weather prayer! I want this snow to stop,' and all that stuff. It was quite a performance.

"Afterward, his aide comes over to him and says, 'General, you know, sometimes your people don't know when you're acting and when you're not.' And Patton's response was just perfect, essentially this: 'It's not important for *them* to know. It's important for *me* to know.'"

Saunders laughed. "So in short, I think a good leader knows when they need to step in and rattle the cage. They need to know, or learn, when to congratulate and when to kick ass," he said. "And aside from all the other things that a leader must be, in whatever way he or she does it, he must be a showman. He must be able to entertain, to grab attention, hold it, and get the message across in a way that people remember it." That could be subtly, overtly, with humor or by somebody else's examples or quotes, he said, and the leader needs to be able to gauge what will be most effective to whom in which situations. "Are good leaders perfect?" Saunders posed. "No, nobody's perfect," he said. "You're going to make mistakes in trying to lead. But the idea that you're willing to get out there and do it again and again and again, regardless of what happens, and to keep going . . . well, your people need to see that you're willing to keep going."

Confidence

In 1974, when Jean Saunders first met the man she would marry a year and a half later, she found him to be "handsome, confident and friendly," she said. Time would prove her husband to be so much more. "He is pretty much an open book," she said of Saunders. "He's funny, compassionate, kind, understanding and knows how to talk to people. He is adventurous, and he's always up for a challenge and loves doing things that others would not do."

That's all endearing and impressive, but ultimately he captured her heart by way of his enduring sense of love, integrity, commitment and persistence. "He is my rock," she said. "He has been there to comfort me and motivate me at times when I really needed him. I feel as though he has always been my protector." Today, the mutual respect, support and devotion is something that neither of them can imagine living without.

Since Jean Saunders began working as director of member relations at Project Lifesaver, she's witnessed first-hand how her husband's character, intentions and interpersonal style extend to impact others. "He cares about people and protecting them," she said. "And when there's a problem, he is the guy who steps up and takes charge. He leads from the front and motivates those around him. And the thing that others may not know is his ability to handle conflict and crisis. He's calm, logical, and keeps those around him confident in their ability to successfully resolve a challenge."

He tries, and it shows. In terms of personifying his own ideals, "I like to think that I'm decent," Saunders said. "But I think that you have to be willing to do it every day and understand that you're going to screw up sometimes. Then, regardless of that, you come back."

His confidence transfers well to his staff. "He doesn't micromanage," Yeaw said of Saunders. Instead, "he is a very effective delegator. He hires proven people, and then he delegates work and he allows them to do their job."

Actually, Carter said, Saunders can leave the micromanagement to him. Carter's style keeps him in the midst of all the minutiae he can handle, so he can help lead as a deportee from "the weeds" in a fashion complementary to Saunders'.

As CEO, Saunders makes the major decisions; "he can't delegate the responsibility," Yeaw assured, "but he can delegate the authority for those people to make decisions that support their progress and run their piece of the organization, their role," he explained. "And he knows, because he knows them, that they will do their job to the best of their ability."

Saunders concurs. "We allow people to do their jobs without sitting on their shoulder," he said. "I like to be able to tell people what I want done and get out of their way, let them do it, let them go. And we give them the ability to do things to make the job better." Saunders assigns the task and the timeline and asks simply to be kept informed. "That way, you're empowering people," he explained. "If they need help or direction, I'm here. And if they can improve something, I tell them, 'Do it! Just let me know what you did; just keep me in the loop.' Because it's amazing what they'll come up with!" he said. He encourages innovative thinking and the willingness to act on self-initiative in the spirit of bettering the organization and its workplace. "You're going to get much better results that way. And hey, some good ideas come out of it, too," he said. And who knows more than a bullheaded lion about the need for freedom within the context of structure?

Flexibility

With all that said, you can't accomplish anything great without some flexibility, Saunders said. "I've been to leadership courses, and I've listened to all the leadership advice, all the models," he said, "but I think much of it boils down to your willingness to adapt. You know, everything doesn't always go the way you want it to go, so you can never turn loose of the *what if, how do, what next,* and *where do we go from here,*" he said. "And you can lay out your plans, but be ready to be adaptable. Because, you know that old adage, 'The best laid plans . . .?' Well, yeah, it's true.

"Because things are always evolving," he continued. "I mean, things are evolving fast. And you've got to have a mindset that *we can make this work.*" Stay on purpose, stay within the guidelines of the mission and its objectives, and listen to the input of others involved;

they may see a way through what the rest of the team perceives as a monumental obstacle. "There may be some compromise to the original plan, but success is not impossible," Saunders said.

"Conversely, don't make changes just because you want to change something," he cautioned. "Any change for the better is pretty much accepted. But change, just for the sake of change, creates resistance. And it can also devalue what you're trying to do because if people don't buy into it and don't embrace it and don't like it, the eventuality is that it's going to bring down the mission.

"Things change," Saunders assured. That's life. "And I have never been one who was resistant to change if it was good change. And if I thought it was horrible change, I'd say so. If I lost, I lost. But you put it out there: 'Hey, you know, this is not working the way it used to, it's got to be changed.'" That's the stuff of progress.

Diplomacy aside, fair warning to anyone inclined to do him wrong: Don't misinterpret the length of his fuse.

"I'm pretty laid back—until you piss me off," Saunders admitted, laughing. "I can get angry quick," he said, "but most of the time it'll have to build up. The main thing that I try to do is get along. Everybody has a point of view, and I don't have to agree with it, I don't have to follow it, but I'm not going to argue them down about it. We all have a point of view, and at some point we either need to change it or live by it, whichever one we choose," he said. Then he rewound briefly to his three-year stint in hell and nodded, with a smirk, "But if you outright screw me, get ready!"

The bottom line on style? According to Saunders, "a good leader is somebody who can get everybody going in the same direction and make them think it was their idea. But they're there to support it," he said. "And they're ready, willing and able to model it. They don't get in the way of it, and they do and say things that inspire people, that make people feel good even in the worst situations. And they support their people and their beliefs.

"And if it's a belief that is destructive, they stand against it," Saunders noted. Good leaders assume the responsibility for steering or redirecting trains of thought that would otherwise undermine confidence and compromise integrity. "They're willing to let their people grow," he said; "they're willing to let their people have an opinion, but if it's destructive, they're going to channel that opinion, and they're going to tell them so: 'We are here for the common good and to accomplish a purpose. If you have a good idea, we welcome it. If it's a destructive idea, I'm going to tell you so. I'm going to keep you on the right path. I'm not going to tell you how to do it, but I'm going to keep you headed in that direction.'"

Essentially, Saunders said, leadership is more about influence and modeling than about forcefulness. Good leaders lead by example.

"You know," he concluded, laughing at the irony, "I feel like I get great results with very little 'leadership.'"

That speaks volumes. He makes leadership look easy—not only to others but even to himself.

TEAMWORK AND CULTURE

Second only to his sense of responsibility, instilled in Saunders as a youth, ranks his early deference to teamwork. The power of working as a team toward a common goal, and of the unanimous acknowledgement that everybody plays a part in the group achieving it, may seem obvious. But if its virtues are taken for granted, hence ignored, rather than the concept being intentionally cultivated, reinforced and regenerated on an ongoing basis, the power is lost. Why put forth so much effort in all other areas of a mission, but fail to infuse purpose, enthusiasm and collective empowerment to the individuals who have chosen to join in pushing that mission forward? They *do* have other options. And that fact is not lost on an effective leader. A good leader knows that. A good leader respects that.

Even amid his primary objectives for the exponential expansion of PLI, Saunders aims conscientiously to fashion and maintain an internal culture where people know they're appreciated for their efforts and contributions, they know they have support when it's needed, and they're valued as much for their fundamental humanity as they are for what they accomplish for the organization.

"I have a tremendous crew," he said of his staff. And it's not the money that attracts them. They come or stay for one reason, he said: "We are doing something good, saving lives, and offering protection."

That's a tall order for a relatively small staff of about fifteen, so to a feasible extent all jobs are everyone's jobs. "We have one clause when we hire them: '...and other duties, as described.' That's in the job description," Saunders said. And while he's upfront about what he expects from his staff, he and Carter both subscribe to the style of leadership by example: "I'm not going to ask anybody to do anything that I wouldn't do myself, or that I am not going to pitch in and help them do.

"Again, that comes back from the military," Saunders said. "And I think that enables people—or maybe it motivates them—to reason that 'if the chief of staff or the CEO can do this, I can do it. If it's not beneath them, it's not beneath me.' I'm very into military leaders, because they act under extreme pressure. They're in combat. One of the things Hal Moore always said—and I've always believed in this— was to cross-train your people. Everybody knows everybody's job so you can step in and do anything. That's just the way it is; when you have things that need to be done, you roll up your sleeves and you do it. Whoever's available, and whoever you can get together. It doesn't matter what your job title or your job description is, you just do it.

"The bottom line is that it's good for the organization, and it's good for the members. And who are the final recipients? The people we're trying to protect," Saunders said. "So all of it just kind of mish-mashes together, and if you want it to work you just get in there and do it."

For all the hard work and intermittent frustration, the overall sense of pride and purpose and the knowledge that they're "making a difference" prevail. Even if Saunders could pay his team more, money couldn't buy that internal gratification. But the devotion is not overlooked.

"Lord knows, we can't pay them what they're worth," Carter said. "They clearly have a drive that makes them want to stay in and push and work, because the demands are constant. I think it's a commitment to see this survive and go forward." Carter recalled PLI having applied for a DOJ (US Department of Justice) grant around 2005. "The auditors were so impressed," he said. "They couldn't believe that we were doing what we were doing with such a small staff." The staff size was about the same in 2017 as it had been back then, and each department—training, logistics, finance and equipment—is still extremely busy and thus completely integral to the operation. "That's what makes it impressive," he said. "Everybody has to be operating extra efficiently to be able to pull this off."

Saunders is big on rewarding and sustaining that morale. When the office receives after-action reports from PLI-affiliated agencies, he circulates them among his staff. He does the same with PLI-related news alerts picked up from throughout North America. The broader a person's perspective about the ripples that he or she makes, the more balanced a perspective one tends to maintain regarding the important things in life—in this case, purpose, mission and teamwork.

"I think that it's important for them to know that whatever they're doing here is having an impact," Saunders said. "You know, you may be the person who puts the equipment together, and if you didn't put that equipment together, this person wouldn't have been saved."

As board chairman, Derus sees a side of Saunders that the public rarely does. Despite the pressures of running such a large nonprofit agency, and how adept Saunders is, "He is always personable and willing to help out any one of his employees," Derus said. "He is also highly motivational to his workforce, which despite its small size continues to work in the background diligently to support his mission." Success in that realm is impressive enough, and it's easy to assume that he'd have to have a militant mindset to achieve it. Yet Saunders could be perceived as an enigma for his paradoxical nature. While his bullheaded persona may appear to dominate, "he also promotes a family-type atmosphere and truly is a caring and compassionate leader," Derus said.

General communication is also key to good teamwork, and phone, Skype and email all support correspondence between PLI's Virginia and Florida offices. But there's nothing quite like the energy exchanged between teammates in-person, face-to-face.

Once a year, Saunders brings them all together for an extended weekend retreat, alternating locations between the two states. This builds camaraderie among staff as they get to know one another on a personal basis, socializing and sharing ideas, concerns, laughter, downtime and leisurely activities. Discussion-wise it is formal, and no relevant topic is taboo. "This is your bitch session," Saunders tells them. "I want to hear all your bitches, all your moaning, all your groaning. But when we come out of here, I want us to have a united front, and I want to hear things that you feel like are going to improve this organization so that we can look at them." He can't promise to follow up with every good idea immediately, especially those that'll cost money, but he considers them all and appreciates the thought and care behind them. The cost of the annual long weekend is always minimal, he said, and "a great investment."

Saunders values the staff's intelligent input and steadfast efforts like a prize. And, as with all other resources, he seeks to protect and optimize these contributions for all their operational and growth potential. To boot, he knows that while purpose and passion have ignited missions for eons, a mission absent of structure quickly reverts back to nothing more than an idea that may or may not ever burgeon. Hence, he institutes a structured system of regiment, rank, and chain of command to support the organization's goals. It's this tightly constructed pipeline that facilitates the flow of synergy and efficiency that has held Project Lifesaver together through the tough times, and advanced its mission to extraordinary successes over the long term.

In short, Saunders strives to recreate for his staff the elements of his own formative years that were essential to his development as an effective team member and leader. Sure, good leaders are purposeful, driven, tenacious, decisive and then some, he concluded; but they're also avid teammates. And if they're *really* wise, "they look out for their people."

PARACHUTE PACKERS

"When you accept leadership, you have to understand that when things come crashing down, they're going to come crashing down on you," Saunders said. "And you'd better have a good support system, because nobody can handle it all alone.

"So as you go along, try to surround yourself with positive people who are willing to put in the effort to make the mission succeed," he advises, "because it isn't going to come easy. Nobody's going to hand things to you. Right now, nobody's handing us anything," he said; "we're still fighting and scrapping and moving ahead.

"And you've got to have somebody who's there to watch your back and to take up the slack," he continued. Carter has been that guy for years. "He's very organized; he's very concise and detail-oriented," Saunders said. "We complement each other, and that's the kind of thing it takes if you want a good organization." Like-minds applied in different ways: "I think that's what makes it run so well."

Carter has been fully committed, and especially during the brutal years. "I'm a reactive person, and I looked at that as us being attacked from the outside," he recalled. "I was going to protect the program. That's my purpose. And I function best when I'm pushed up against a wall," he said. "And we've had a couple of times like that," Carter noted, "but we've survived, endeavored, and we've moved forward." Yet his depth of devotion to PLI has a lot to do with Saunders. In terms of employers, "I want somebody who has a goal and a vision and has a commitment to something great," he said. "When I have that type of situation to work with, I'll give 200 percent."

For all the support and faith of every person, group and organization that has delivered it since the conception of Project Lifesaver, Saunders speaks his eternal gratitude. If not for them . . . *who knows*?

Beginning with Nancy Gray and Pilot International, Sheriff Newhart and Dave Newby, the City of Chesapeake, and of course Chesapeake General Hospital's charitable foundation that funded Project Lifesaver's pilot program way back when, "We couldn't have done it without all of them," Saunders affirmed. "And of course, a number of the member agencies have shown tremendous support over the years, morally, and when we were having a tough time, sticking with us and supporting us even during lowest points," he said. "Let's face it: They could have jumped ship in the tough times. But they stayed with us. They supported us. They helped keep us with our head above water," he said. "I'll always be grateful to all of them, because without them, we wouldn't be here. Had they not stayed with us in the hard times, we wouldn't be here."

Even today, Saunders says, "knowing that these agencies are hanging with us, and they're going to be there for the duration, gives us a lot of motivation to keep pushing. Following the situations that we had years ago, if agencies had just said, 'Well, we're leaving, that's it, we've had enough,' after a while we'd have had to ask, 'Why are we doing this, why are we fighting so hard?' To me, their support is immeasurable."

While every single Project Lifesaver agent, volunteer and proponent has played a significant role in the growth and development of the organization, those closest to him have helped Saunders develop as its leader. "They're my best critics," Saunders said. "They'll tell me in a minute if they think something's screwed up. And that's as necessary as anybody patting you on the back," he said. "If you're screwing up, sometimes you need to go back and rethink some things." And for the sake of the organization and everyone involved, "I will," he said.

To all of them, and on behalf of every person ever to be rescued by the program that runs on the fuel of their devotion, Saunders owes a piece of his heart.

And as for his wife, Jean, he can hardly express the depth of his love and thanks for her having been his rock, his inspiration, his motivation, and his all-essential constant through it all.

But he does his best to show it, and it's evident in everything he does, she said.

FAITH, SPIRITUALITY AND INTUITION

Chuck O'Connor recalled the days when he and other members of his Navy SEAL team provided military-type training to Saunders' SWAT unit. As the primary point of contact for that SEAL exchange team, O'Connor also participated in SWAT operations. He was immediately impressed by Saunders' leadership style and the depth of "sincere respect" that Saunders' men had for their commander, but O'Connor also noticed elements of a more empathic, even spiritual, nature in him—something rarely observable in that line of work, yet undeniably constant, pervasive and deep-rooted in Saunders.

"Gene has respect for all life," he said. "And he had incredible instincts understanding the nature of individuals willing to commit violent crime." Therefore, he noted, "his tactical planning and operational leadership was not limited to the obvious crime committed, but always displayed compassion and spiritual presence not typically associated with violent crime response.

"His tactical solutions and leadership always quickly resolved very violent encounters with the minimal use of force," O'Connor continued. "His strength was his ability to focus on an appropriate tactical response to the violent threat conditions while preserving the reputation of the police department, all staff personnel, and the positive perception by political leaders and citizens in Chesapeake that their police department performed with honor." The same threads of purpose, responsibility and humanitarianism ran through Saunders' leadership in the Civil Air Patrol, O'Connor attested. "Serving the public as a peace officer did not end after the day," he said. "His leadership and infantry field craft skills were an important addition to the rescue mission of the CAP. And his compassion for all life is his drive for his dedication to be there during times of crisis and emergency."

Saunders doesn't consider himself religious, per se. He believes in God, although his parents hadn't been notably religious, regular church-going people. Yet he does possess a strong sense of spirituality, and that fortifies his earthly experience. It's an empowering loop of faith in a higher power and faith in himself. How much of it is innate and how much of it did he learn? "Who knows?" he admits. But he believes it's a combination.

His belief in God is inborn, he said. And certainly the experiences that he was fortunate to have during his formative and career years were serious confidence builders, but only because he had seized those opportunities, acted on a belief that they had value, and chosen to pursue them with a plan for personal excellence. Personal achievement reinforces leadership aptitude on many levels.

But what is the seed of the underlying self-esteem and inherent drive that precede one's willingness to try . . . and try again . . . and again?

"I think everybody needs to develop, or should have, some sense of self-worth," Saunders said. "And then, what is your purpose in life?

"I think everybody has a purpose," he continued. "It's whether or not they want to find it and run with it. Do I think everybody has one single purpose? Well, I think God gave you the ability to have different purposes, and then it's a matter of which ones a person chooses to channel. You know," he clarified, "whatever your talent, or your psyche, or your intelligence is, what is your interest?" And your intention?

And without faith internal, how can a person extend faith in others enough to trust, delegate, and team up in the spirit of purpose, mission and perseverance? Moreover, what would become of the extent of faith in others that's so critical, yet so often elusive, in the wake of the destruction wrought by betrayal?

"Some people talk about reincarnation," Saunders said. "My wife, Jean, she's a firm believer in reincarnation. And I have to lean that way, too," he said before further validating the idea with accounts of one of his personal heroes.

"General Patton firmly believed that he had been a warrior all his life—and even before," in past lives, Saunders explained. "Now, is that true? I don't know," he said. "But does it have some validity? I can't say that it doesn't."

Saunders referenced a story that has documented Patton's leaning in print and film accounts.

"Patton was in Europe during World War II, and he and his Jeep driver were driving along, and he told the driver, 'Turn here.' And another general who was with him said 'That's not the way to the battlefield, it's over here.' And Patton said, 'No, turn here.' So they turned down this road, and they got to the end of it, and there was this big field. And he said, 'This was a battlefield.' And the other general said 'How do you know?' And Patton said, 'Because I was here.' And he described the battle, and who fought." That battle had occurred many years prior to Patton's birth.

Saunders believes that there's so much more to the blueprints that people bring into the world—so much more evidence to support the weight of nature over nurture, considering the inherent wisdom, the sense of purpose, and the interests that drive us—than people seem to consider. Some of us never remember *not* knowing or being something, as if we're born with certain knowledge and past experience. "Why do I even believe in God?" he posed. "I don't know; I just do.

"And I don't know whether I'm correct or not correct about reincarnation," Saunders continued, "but it's just an innate feeling that everything in the past got me to where I am now. You know, all the things that I've done in past lives, whatever it was, that had to have something to do with what I do and how I am right now." To those who dismiss the possibility, "I submit this," he said: "Why have I always had such a big interest in the military, and *been* in the military? Why have I always had such a big interest in law enforcement, and *been* in law enforcement? Why have I always had this innate sense of serving? That's not something that my parents taught me. Where did I get it from? I think it came with the package. So, if somebody were to ask me, 'What do you think you did in past lives?' Well, I was either a military soldier or I was a cop. You know, I think I served the same way I am now in all my previous lives, in some capacity."

Saunders' own expectation of his personal performance has always been his nature. To him, it was a given. He never questioned it, nor did he see it as necessarily extraordinary. But to so many others, it's truly remarkable.

O'Connor recalled the consensus from the years of the SWAT-SEAL training exchange initiated and upheld by Saunders. "All of us were always impressed, after an operation, by how smoothly the operation unfolded," O'Connor said. "We also knew that success was directly related to Gene." They took note of his excellence at identifying the needs of others and taking the lead to create solutions.

Saunders has long been recognized by many for exceptionalism under pressure and in crisis. He becomes super-calm and -logical, others tell him, but he's never thought about it as anything out of the ordinary, he said. "So there again," he has to question, "where did that come from? I don't know. Do you train people to be super-calm? I don't think you can. You can train them in what to do, but they have to train themselves to be super-calm, or they are calm by nature. I've never had a problem with being calm in crisis.

"So if reincarnation is true," Saunders said, "and I have no reason to disbelieve it, I think that I am the sum of the parts of every time I've been here previously. And I think that that goes with you to the next life, however many times you come back."

One thing he's had to further develop in this life is trust in his gut instincts. Looking back, Saunders said he'd realized a little too late that he could have put the old cop hackles to better use in the nonprofit world. He just hadn't realized how essential that gut instinct would be in the underbelly afterlife.

"As we got deeper into Project Lifesaver," Saunders recalled, "and it became more successful, and we brought more people into it, I probably wasn't as cautious as I should have been. We had our eye on the prize, and we were moving forward, and we were actually moving very fast," he said. "When it first started, it was like a locomotive." Part of what enables that to happen is leadership with a positive mindset, so Saunders hadn't been anticipating any negative events he had been trained to watch for in his previous career, and especially not events deliberately created by people he trusted. "I brought some people on board, and unfortunately, they betrayed me," he said. It was a hard lesson in the importance of trusting your gut, he admitted.

Now, Saunders' advice for others includes keeping this unfortunate reality on their radar. "If something doesn't feel right, it's not right," he asserts. Sometimes good people are inclined to offer too much benefit of the doubt, too much tolerance of questionable behavior, he explained. They project their own good character and high moral standards onto others, assuming the principles are automatically shared by all who seem to be striving in a common cause. But it's worth reevaluating that inclination. Trust your instincts more, Saunders advises. "You know, in some situations, you don't need to go find out all about what's wrong with it. Step back, look at it, assess it to an appropriate extent, and if it doesn't feel right, find another way."

He believes in God. He also believes in Jesus as Christ. "And I guess maybe I'm weird," Saunders added, "but do I believe in angels? Yes. Guardian angels? Yes, I do," he said.

Saunders believes that everyone has a guardian angel and that he probably has several. "I must have," he said laughing, "Because I'm still here! Either that, or I've got a very active one. If I didn't, I wouldn't be here right now, sure of that. There've been too many times where, you know . . . there's just been too many times."

This evolution of the spirit has always been an assumption, a part of life, for him. And while he's not a churchgoer, he does pray. "It may be an inner prayer; it may be a silent prayer; it may be a whispered prayer," he said. "But yeah, I pray. I prayed a lot during all this stuff that was going on in those toughest years. Do I still pray? Absolutely. For guidance and being able to make the right decisions, and for strength, absolutely.

"I think you need to have faith in whatever god there is," Saunders said. "Regarding the Big Bang theory, I don't believe in that. I believe that there is some supreme being, and that we are here for a purpose, and I believe that everybody has a purpose." Whether or not an individual strives to fulfill that purpose is a matter of choice, he said.

"I also firmly believe that everything that happens, happens for a reason," Saunders continued. "And I believe that people come into your life at certain times for a reason." Now, what do you do with it when it happens? When a new door opens, what are you going to do with it? Are you going to walk through it? Are you going to close it? What are you gonna do with it? "I think God gave us the ability to make choices. So, do you make a good choice or a bad choice? And do I think that every opportunity in the world that a person has, they're able to take advantage of it?" he asked. "No," he reasoned, "because sometimes we don't recognize the opportunity." As for people who are downtrodden, "a lot of that is bad choices," Saunders said. Comparing people who exist with essentially equal resources in essentially equal circumstances—good and bad—what's the difference between those who do well in life and those who get buried by it, if it's not because of the decisions they make? And countless people overcome great adversity and odds that others consider extreme, he noted. "Why?" he asked. "Because they believed in themselves, they believed in God, and they believed that they could come out of it. And they didn't quit." It's like climbing a ladder out of the pits: Step by step, rung by rung, you ascend, he said.

Again, Saunders can't explain the origin of his unwavering faith. He and Jean discuss these things frequently, and their thought provocation and open-mindedness is important to both of them. "I've never been a student of it; I've never had anybody try to teach it to me," he said. "So where'd I get it from? I had to have had something in my past that I am not conscious of that brought all of this into light, and here it is."

Many refer to Saunders an "angel on Earth." Those who don't subscribe to the concept of the supernatural could simply pose the question, 'With allies like him, who needs angels?'

But the magic of it makes complete sense to former SEAL O'Connor. "When he explained to me that he'd started Project

Lifesaver, I was not surprised at all," he said of Saunders. "The current success story of Project Lifesaver will live beyond all of us because of Gene's vision and inspiration."

Regardless of the forces behind it, *there's* a testament to an *afterlife*.

FOURTEEN

The Ripple Effect

"I believe the future is excellent."

—Chief Gene Saunders, founder and CEO,
Project Lifesaver International

A s of January 2019, Project Lifesaver International consisted of approximately 1,600 agencies throughout North America and had completed 3,512 search-and-rescue events for PLI clients. All were successful.

Recent years have seen significant strides in technology. Aside from the new drones, advancements include improvements to receivers and antennas, making them smaller, more sensitive, lighter and easier to handle. PLI now also offers a perimeter system, which alerts caregivers if a client ventures beyond a designated boundary.

Looking ahead, "I believe the future is excellent," Saunders said. He plans to continue developing and offering the best technology possible, and also to further develop the Alzheimer's and autism training programs. "These populations are getting larger," he said, "and the demand on public safety to respond to these incidents is only going to increase. So I want Project Lifesaver to constantly evolve and get better. I want it to excel. I want to keep driving forward, and keep finding ways to do it better, faster and more easily, so that whenever these guys go out to do a search—while nothing in life is 100-percent guaranteed—they can be ninety-nine-percent confident that they're going to get a successful search."

With all this drive, will Saunders ever retire? "Yeah, I'm sure," he said, shrugging, "when they carry me out, probably. It's just like my wife said when I retired from SWAT: 'You know, you've done all of this, you've been on all of these missions, and all these things have been successful. At some point, somebody else has to take over. Do you want it to be because they pushed you to go? Or do you want it to be because you went out a winner?'" He prefers to go on his own schedule, although with so much more to do, he's in no hurry. But when he's moved on, he hopes this spirit will hang around indefinitely: "I want Project Lifesaver to do what it is intended to do and do it better than anybody else," he said.

The ultimate reward for Saunders is impact. "I know this is a cliché," he said, "but the one thing that I've always wanted to feel is that whatever I did, however small it was, or whatever small part it played, that it made a difference; that it accomplished something that altered or changed something or made a difference to somebody. Even if it was only one person."

Jean Saunders shares her husband's sense of personal satisfaction. "When I work conferences, to hear the police officers and deputies come up to my husband and thank him for this wonderful program, what better measurement of success can you get?" she asked. In the end, she knows that nothing else he has done will compare to the impact he's made on the lives of others in immeasurable—as well as measurable—ways.

Saunders said he tears up with sentiment fairly easily these days, now that he no longer has to switch off his emotions. In citing examples of sentimental triggers, he made his final military reference—a scene from the movie "Saving Private Ryan."

"The closing scene is what really got me," Saunders said. "Boy, I lost it." He teared up as he began to describe the portrayal of the sentiment of a warrior in his later stage of life:

"He goes down on his knee, and he asks his wife, 'Have I been a good man?'" Saunders pressed his lips closed, threw up his hand and shrugged. "That was it," he said, "it gets me every time."

Perhaps Saunders asks the same question of himself. And if the sentiments of Amber Williams, a retired Virginia police sergeant and now a volunteer with Project Lifesaver International, would be any affirmation, her answer is a resounding, "Yes!

"I think of him every time I help a Project Lifesaver agency or client," Williams said. And as the daughter of a man living with Alzheimer's disease, her own heavy heart is supported by the knowledge that "if the time ever comes that we need Project Lifesaver, I'm confident Dad will be found." Her internal torment by the disease's impact on her father can best be expressed by the lyrics of *A Thousand Goodbyes*, a song she wrote for him:

A THOUSAND GOODBYES

By Amber Williams

I know he sees me
But I don't know if it's me
Or someone else locked in a memory.
I hope he's happy, when he thinks about his life,
Remembers the good times with his children and his wife.
(Chorus)
I feel so helpless when I look into his eyes
It feels like he is giving me a thousand goodbyes.
Goodbye.
The tears start flowing as my heart breaks inside.
Goodbye.

The road ahead is somewhere I don't want to go
The more it's traveled, the more I feel alone.
Piece by Piece the memories disappear
Days turn into months, and months turn into years

(Repeat chorus)

Pictures from the past
Have him traveling fast
To places from long, long ago.
His nights are now his days

As he wanders away
I don't know which way to go.

A thousand goodbyes
Oh... A thousand goodbyes...
I know he sees me, but I don't know if it's me.
Please don't go (whispered).

© Amber Hayes Williams

The song can be found on YouTube by typing "A Thousand Goodbyes by Amber Williams" into the site's search bar. Williams performs it live each year at the Project Lifesaver International annual conference, and attendees would be hard-pressed to find a dry eye by the end. Everyone in the room knows the beast.

It's the least she can contribute to the congregation, Williams said. "Every day," she explained, "I thank God for Chief Saunders."

Back at the Virginia Beach oceanfront, Bob Smith said that as a Project Lifesaver client, he feels safer. His mother said, "He is."

Smith pondered what floats his boat these days. "Swimming, when it's nice and warm," he said. "Chilly weather, basketball," and keeping the workplace "clean and safe" for his cherished co-workers. He loves bakeries and hopes to someday work in that industry, alongside others who have autism.

Life's good for Smith: *Simple. Peaceful. Transcendent of the once-predominant beast of search-and-rescue "failure."*

To Saunders, who deploys parachutes high above the earth, just to savor the serenity as the wind ripples through a canopy, peace and simplicity are the glory of the conquest.

CPSIA information can be obtained
at www.ICGtesting.com
Printed in the USA
BVHW030958140519
548238BV00007B/114/P